COACH WOODEN'S PYRAMID OF SUCCESS

Coach Wooden is the "winningest" coach I have ever known in the profession. The way he took great players and molded them into national champions with a sprinkling of overachievers is spectacular. When I read his book, I knew exactly where he got his wisdom.

John's confidence, poise, communication skills and patience come from the Lord. He allowed these to enfold him, and the results show in this book.

BOBBY BOWDEN
HEAD FOOTBALL COACH, FLORIDA STATE UNIVERSITY

Reading *Coach Wooden's Pyramid of Success* by Jay Carty and Coach Wooden made me feel like I was back at Coach's home, when a warm, peaceful feeling would come over me as I listened to Coach talk in his easy manner. Jay brings together Coach's faith and hard work and intertwines them with principles from the Bible. Just like Coach, this book is easy to be with, and reading it brings a sense of peace.

ANN MEYERS DRYSDALE
UCLA ALL-AMERICAN
HALL OF FAMER
OLYMPIAN

This truly inspirational book shows us how Coach Wooden has used his faith as a cornerstone to live his life. Like the great teacher and coach that he is, Coach Wooden challenges us to evaluate where we stand on fundamental principles and gives us guidance to improve in these areas of our lives.

RUTH RILEY
WNBA DETROIT SHOCK
2004 OLYMPIC GOLD MEDALIST

For years, Fellowship of Christian Athletes has been privileged to be associated with Coach John Wooden. He has been one of FCA's cornerstone coaches, and each year we honor him during the NCAA Men's Final Four Legends of the Hardwood Breakfast by presenting an award in his name. Coach exemplifies FCA's core values of Integrity, Serving, Teamwork and Excellence, which have been the building blocks of our ministry for more than 50 years. Many times Coach has encouraged and challenged us, not only with his stories of success, but also with his great model of faith. I pray that you will use this powerful book to learn from Coach Wooden that the secret of success ultimately comes from the Master Coach—Jesus Christ.

LES STECKEL
PRESIDENT AND CHIEF EXECUTIVE OFFICER
FELLOWSHIP OF CHRISTIAN ATHLETES

Coach Wooden taught us everything from how to put on our shoes and socks before a game to how to build a foundation for life based on human values and personal characteristics. He showed us how to win championships, but all along he was also teaching us the underlying themes of his core as a human being— his Pyramid of Success. Some of us were slow learners, but learn we did. We learned how to think, how to dream, how to develop our skills, how to make decisions and how to achieve peak performance. The principles that worked when I was at UCLA many years ago still work today. At 94, Coach is still teaching. In this new book, he goes deep into each point of the Pyramid and offers fresh challenges for us all to be the best we can be.

BILL WALTON
SPORTS COMMENTATOR
THREE-TIME UCLA ALL-AMERICAN
NBA HALL OF FAMER AND NBA MVP

At 94, Coach is still growing and still teaching. To my mind, Coach Wooden always stopped slightly before the question, Faith in what? was answered. This book takes that step and makes the Pyramid more majestic than ever.

PAUL WESTPHAL
HEAD BASKETBALL COACH, PEPPERDINE UNIVERSITY

For seven years, I have been waiting for Coach Wooden to write in detail about his famous Pyramid of Success. Finally, Coach has done it with his gifted writing partner, Jay Carty, and the wait has been well worth it. This is a powerful combination of practical life lessons and deep spiritual truths that you can apply to your daily life. I highly recommend this book for people of all ages.

PAT WILLIAMS
SENIOR VICE PRESIDENT, ORLANDO MAGIC

Coach Wooden is an inspiration to everyone, not just to coaches. His Pyramid of Success is very thought-provoking and could be used by anyone in any business in a very positive way.

ROY WILLIAMS
HEAD BASKETBALL COACH, UNIVERSITY OF NORTH CAROLINA

Coach Wooden's Pyramid of Success, written with Jay Carty, is loaded with wisdom, common sense and everyday practicality. It's a road map for living well and finishing well.

ZIG ZIGLAR
AUTHOR AND MOTIVATIONAL SPEAKER/TEACHER

COACH
WOODEN'S
PYRAMID
OF
SUCCESS

.

COACH WOODEN'S PYRAMID OF SUCCESS

JOHN WOODEN
JAY CARTY

Regal

From Gospel Light
Ventura, California, U.S.A.

PUBLISHED BY REGAL BOOKS
FROM GOSPEL LIGHT
VENTURA, CALIFORNIA, U.S.A.
Regal PRINTED IN THE U.S.A.

Regal Books is a ministry of Gospel Light, a Christian publisher dedicated to serving the local church. We believe God's vision for Gospel Light is to provide church leaders with biblical, user-friendly materials that will help them evangelize, disciple and minister to children, youth and families.

It is our prayer that this Regal book will help you discover biblical truth for your own life and help you meet the needs of others. May God richly bless you.

For a free catalog of resources from Regal Books/Gospel Light, please call your Christian supplier or contact us at 1-800-4-GOSPEL *or* www.regalbooks.com.

The Pyramid of Success®

Cover design by David Griffing
Interior design by Stephen Hahn
Edited by Steven Lawson

Library of Congress Cataloging-in-Publication Data
Wooden, John R.
  Coach Wooden's pyramid of success / John R. Wooden and Jay Carty.
    p. cm.
  Includes bibliographical references.
  ISBN 0-8307-3679-4—ISBN 0-8307-3718-9 (trade pbk.)
  1. Success—Religious aspects—Christianity. I. Carty, Jay. II. Title.

BV4598.3.W66 2005
248.4—dc22   2004030016

2   3   4   5   6   7   8   9   10   11   12   13   14   15   /   11   10   09   08   07

Rights for publishing this book in other languages are contracted by Gospel Light Worldwide, the international nonprofit ministry of Gospel Light. Gospel Light Worldwide also provides publishing and technical assistance to international publishers dedicated to producing Sunday School and Vacation Bible School curricula and books in the languages of the world. For additional information, visit www.gospellightworldwide.org; write to Gospel Light Worldwide, P.O. Box 3875, Ventura, CA 93006; or send an e-mail to info@gospellightworldwide.org.

DEDICATION

From Coach Wooden
to
the memory of Joshua and Roxie Anna Wooden, my parents

You gave me the foundation upon which I could build my life and
from which I could teach others.

to
the memory of Nell, my beloved wife

You walked each step with me and together we applied the Pyramid
principles in our marriage and in life. I think of you every day.

and to
all of my students

I am proud to see how, over the years, so many of you have
used the building blocks and mortar qualities in the
Pyramid of Success to become the best you can be.

From Jay Carty
to Gary Lydic

You are a trusted friend, a hall-of-fame encourager and an
opener of ministry doors. You are a man who has had my back and a
guard who loves to drive the paint. Dear Gary, thank you for standing
with me all these years. May God keep you and the ones you love free
from fear and harm as He continues to bless you.

CONTENTS

THE FOUNDATION OF A LEGEND

I have always admired John Wooden, not only for his success on the basketball court, but also for his success in creating a legacy of excellence and integrity. When you are in the public eye you are under a great deal of scrutiny, and it is easy to make a major mistake or two. Over all these years, Coach Wooden has upheld his character and ideals in an admirable way. When he is remembered, thoughts will be drawn toward his teams, his attitude and his love for his wife and family.

John Wooden will also be remembered for his teaching ability. They don't call him "Coach" for nothing. His Pyramid of Success has been the cornerstone of his teaching for many years.

In this book, Coach Wooden and Jay Carty take you through Scriptures and show you the tremendous practicality of Scriptures in your life today. They show you how to use God's Word to build a solid foundation in your life for whatever you do.

All good and lasting success is based on how we relate to God and how we relate to our fellow man. I hope that as you read this book, you will begin to understand what has served as the foundation for a great sportsman and a great human being.

David Robinson
San Antonio Spurs, 1989-2003
Two-Time NBA World Champion

ACKNOWLEDGMENTS

Special thanks from
Jay Carty
to
Sam Talbert

My "Main-Man Sam" is a mainstay in the One-on-One series. He is great at dreaming up biblical applications, choosing verses, making sure that I don't make doctrinal mistakes and keeping me from being too edgy. Sam, I don't know what I would do without you. You know the Bible better than anyone else I know. Thanks again, Sam.

Thanks from Coach Wooden and Jay Carty
to
the entire Regal team for going the extra mile.

Our publisher, Bill Greig III, believed in this project and gave us the vision to make it happen. The art team of Robert Williams, David Griffing and Steve Hahn created another exceptional layout and cover. Our editor, Steven Lawson, was firm and thorough as he exercised his outstanding talents to help us make this a better book. Bill Denzel, Bill Schultz, Marlene Baer, Kim Bangs, Jennifer Cullis, Deena Davis, Nola Grunden, Jessica Jones, Carole Maurer, Bethany Watts, Hillary Wiens, the sales team and so many others at Regal Books put forth their best efforts to help make this book the best it could be.

DEFINING SUCCESS

By Coach John R. Wooden

It all started at Martinsville High School in Indiana. When we were sophomores, a teacher assigned us to write a paper on the definition of success. Many of my classmates equated success with wealth, fame, power and status; others characterized it as the winning of championships. I wasn't comfortable with any of these descriptions and began to mull over what the word really means.

Many years later, after I had graduated from Purdue University, I became a teacher and again had to give the concept of success some serious thought. Some of the parents at South Bend Central High School, where I taught, presented a problem. They wanted their average children to get only As and Bs—they considered a lower grade as failure. A grade of C was good enough for someone else's children, but not for their own. (Of course, years later when I had children, grandchildren and great-grandchildren of my own, I understood this sentiment.)

However, as an educator, I differed with the parents' reasoning, and I could not embrace their measurement regarding success and failure. It seemed unfair to consider a student with average ability who performed to the best of his or her ability as a failure simply because he or she was not at the top of the class. Moreover, it was not right for me, as a teacher, to give a grade that was undeserved. Faced with this dilemma, I continued in my quest to define success. Wanting to have an impact on my students, I sought to identify the principles that would serve them for a lifetime.

I knew what success was not. I didn't see recommendations, promotions, points, scores, trophies, medals or money as accurate measurements. Such items may result in status, but status isn't necessarily success.

So how could I define success? I began with two principles my dad had passed along to my brothers and me when we were boys growing up on a farm.

1. Don't try to be better than someone else.
2. Always try to be the best you can be.

Dad reasoned that whether we were better than someone else should not be a focus because our position in relation to others was out of our control. We could not control another's performance, nor could we control how we would be ranked. All we could do was our best. While dad urged us to always learn from other people, he also cautioned us against depending upon others to define our self-worth or success. Instead, he wanted us to try very hard to give the best possible effort to become the best we could be and let the results take care of themselves.

A poem helped further my understanding of doing one's best.

At God's footstool to confess,
A poor soul knelt and bowed his head.
"I failed." he cried. The Master said,
"Thou didst thy best, that is success."[1]

I don't know who wrote these verses, but the underlying message helped me identify one of the core ingredients of success and has had a lasting impact on my life.

In 1934, having been influenced by these wise words from my dad and this poem, I penned a definition of success that has stood the test of time:

Success is peace of mind that is the direct result of self-satisfaction in knowing you did your best to become the best that you are capable of becoming.

Within this framework, each person becomes the only one who can ultimately judge his or her own success.

You are the only one who knows whether you have won.

I always wanted my students to know that it was up to each of them to become as good as they could become with the gifts and talents they had been given and in the circumstances in which they found themselves. God made each of us unique. Each one of us has a different mix of talents and a distinctive set of circumstances. In this context, each of us can learn to make the best effort we are capable of making, which may include changing some of our circumstances, if possible. If we refrain from comparing ourselves to others and stay off other people's ladders of success, we will have peace of mind. If we put forward our best effort, we can consider ourselves to be successful.

As I developed the principles that I would eventually use in my Pyramid, I researched what others had said about success. I came across one definition that illustrated the pursuit of success with a ladder. The idea of a ladder made me think of a pyramid. In expanding my definition of success, I decided to use building blocks of personal qualities. When we build from a wide foundation upwards to an apex, we end up with a pyramid. Thus, the idea for the Pyramid of Success was born.

It took many years to settle upon the makeup I now use in the Pyramid. Many times I altered the content and location of specific building blocks—except for the cornerstones of the foundation (industriousness and enthusiasm) and the qualities at the top (faith and patience). These four principles have never changed. I'm content with the Pyramid as it is presented in this book.

Today, in sports and in most areas of life, many people adopt a win-at-all-costs stance. Our media and popular culture bolster this approach. However, as you will see, much of what I teach takes a different slant. I maintain that there is no end to living a win-at-all-costs life and, when we follow this course, we find that we have no peace of mind.

What I offer here are the keys to obtaining a peace of mind that is the direct result of the self-satisfaction achieved when you know that you did your best to become the best that you are capable of becoming.

BUILDING THE PYRAMID

By Jay Carty

Coach John Wooden has enjoyed legendary success as the greatest coach of the twentieth century and one of the most revered teachers of all time. At the time of this writing, he is 94, but the only thing old about him is his body. Despite Coach's age, he seems to have boundless energy. At a time when he could relax and savor his success, instead his mind is always working, and he constantly challenges others with new ideas. Coach maintains a personal appearance schedule that tires me just to think about it, even though I am 30 years younger than he is.

Coach's Pyramid of Success is one of the most popular and effective motivational tools around. Corporations use it. Speakers laud it. Books have been written about it. Coach still speaks about it as often as he can. Many of Coach's former players attest that as young men the Pyramid's building blocks provided them with a foundation and helped mold them as they became adults. To this day, quite a few—including Bill Walton and Kareem Abdul-Jabbar—point to the Pyramid as a key to their personal success, both on and off the basketball court.

Coach Wooden's Pyramid of Success has been copied, plagiarized and pirated. That's been mostly okay with Coach. He feels honored that it helps others reach the apex of success, even if he does not always get the credit.

Why a pyramid?

In recent years, pyramids (along with triangles, pentagrams and rainbows) have often been linked to the New Age movement. Be assured that Coach Wooden's use of the pyramid (which is also in the shape of a triangle) had nothing to do with the New Age revival of the late twentieth century. For Coach, the pyramid offers a simple way to visualize the foundation and important building blocks of a successful life.

Today a plethora of motivational devices, speakers and philosophies flood the marketplace. Some of these concepts rely on hype; others promote a variation of the you-too-can-be-God mind-set; most depend on positive thinking and self-talk that falls into the hocus-pocus, mumbo-jumbo trap. The Pyramid of Success is also a motivational tool, but different from all others. Coach developed the building blocks and mortar (values he lists on the sides of the Pyramid) to stand biblical scrutiny—and it passes with flying colors.

The principles laid down in the Bible produce good in people and societies. For example, if enough people practiced Christian ethics today, both believers and nonbelievers could leave their homes unlocked, a handshake would be better than a contract, and young children could safely play in neighborhood parks. Why? Biblical truth works if people apply it in their lives, whether or not the people are followers of Jesus Christ. Since the Pyramid of Success contains biblical principles, its application is limitless.

Coach Wooden taught the principles to his basketball players, but the principles work for anyone and in any setting. They will benefit students, mothers, cooks, lawyers, taxi drivers, politicians, dental hygienists, stockbrokers, farmers—the discipline or occupation does not matter. They will even work for athletes who become pastors or work in ministry. In the appendices of this book, read how the Pyramid's principles helped shape the lives of former UCLA Bruin players Jack Arnold, Ralph Drollinger, Doug McIntosh and Willie Naulls, each of whom are now in full-time Christian ministry.

The Pyramid's principles will strengthen corporations, governments, schools, small businesses, nonprofit organizations and religious bodies. They work in the United States, in Great Britain, in Romania, in Kenya, in India, in Venezuela and all over the world. The Pyramid has even been translated into Chinese. And it works for every generation. Coach's oldest great-granddaughter, Cori Nicholson, is an undergraduate student at the University of California at Riverside and uses the Pyramid's principles every day. Turn the page to the special introduction and read her account.

With God's touch, this book can change your life dramatically. It has the potential of facilitating the focus of your life's work and ministry. It can help you maximize your abilities. After reading Coach's words about each building block and each point in the mortar, you will never look at success the same way. I believe the information in this book can be instrumental in helping you to achieve success in all of your endeavors and in life itself.

When Coach presents the Pyramid, he starts at the cornerstones—industriousness and enthusiasm. He then moves toward the apex, one block at a time. Before reaching the top (success), he talks about the mortar elements of faith and patience. In this book, we present daily readings on each building block and each essential quality of the mortar. Because the mortar is what keeps the Pyramid together and runs through all of the building blocks, we will first present the building blocks in order, move on to the mortar and finally arrive at the apex.

Each reading is divided into three parts: First, Coach lays out his time-proven thoughts, often bringing in spiritual elements; I follow with thoughts that help illuminate the biblical context of each building block and mortar quality; then it is your turn. We want to give you the opportunity to build a Pyramid of Success in your life. To help you mix the mortar, lay the foundation and build each block, we have included probing questions, a commitment declaration and a prayer that will help you apply the principles to your life.

You will want to take out a pen and paper (perhaps a journal) and work through each reading. After you answer each question, we hope that you will be bold enough to check each commitment box and say the suggested prayer. Of course, when talking to God, you can add your own thoughts.

May God richly bless you as you ascend Coach Wooden's Pyramid of Success.

Kyle Duncan

Jay and Coach

TEACHING THE GENERATIONS

By Cori Nicholson

"Your great-grandfather is John Wooden! Do you know how cool that is?" This is an exclamation I have heard many times over the last nineteen years. Yes, for the record, John Wooden, the best collegiate basketball coach in history, is my great-grandfather, and yes, I do know how cool that is.

The title "great-grandfather" is somewhat of an understatement, because he is so much more than a great-grandfather. He is one of the greatest people you could ever meet in your entire life. Knowing that I come from his blood is a blessing itself. My name is Cori and I am Papa's oldest great-grandchild. I attend college at the University of California, Riverside, where I practice his Pyramid building blocks every day.

Papa and I have always had a very close relationship. I was born in 1985, about six months after my great-grandmother, Nell Wooden, passed away. (We still call her "Mama.") I think that because I came at a time when he was so deep in sorrow, my birth created a bond between us that can never be broken. The love that we share is immense and I hope that it will last forever.

Many people don't know this, but my Papa is first a teacher and then a coach. When you ask him what he did for a living, he will say that he was a teacher. He has such an amazing passion for teaching. And it has rubbed off on me. I hope to follow in his footsteps, just as my Aunt Cathleen did, and become a teacher as well. I just hope that I can fill their shoes.

Ever since I was a little girl, I have known about the Pyramid of Success. It has always been a part of my life. People probably think that Papa sat us all down as kids and taught us about each of the building blocks of the Pyramid; however, that is not the case. In fact, I don't have any memories of Papa teaching me a lesson straight from the Pyramid. When Papa taught us lessons, it was through stories or by example, never just from the Pyramid. Now that I'm older I realize that he was using the Pyramid to teach us, just in a more subtle way.

The Pyramid is applicable to much more than sports. Frankly, if it only applied to sports, I would have no business writing about it. When it comes to athletic ability, that is the area in which I did not inherit any of Papa's genes. The blocks of the Pyramid are a form of moral guideline by which everyone should strive to live. The two blocks that have affected my life the most are "enthusiasm" and "competitive greatness."

Enthusiasm—Brushes off upon those with whom you come in contact. You must truly enjoy what you are doing.

I am probably one of the most enthusiastic people that you could ever meet. This is a big part of my life. I show enthusiasm every day that I go to school. If you aren't enthusiastic about what you're doing, how do you expect to get it done? College is a place where enthusiasm is crucial. If you don't like what you're studying, and you can't find something to be enthusiastic about, then it will be a grueling place. Papa and the rest of my family have always taught me to make the best out of whatever happens. If you find the good things and are enthusiastic about them, then everything will be okay.

The other block that has greatly affected my life is "competitive greatness," not in sports, but in life.

Competitive Greatness—Be at your best when your best is needed. Enjoyment of a difficult challenge.

This block applies to my life mostly in school, but in other areas too. I have to be at my best in order to pass my classes, get good grades and obtain my degree. The goals that I have set in this regard are going to be difficult to achieve, so I must enjoy the challenges. I also apply this block in my relationships with my family and friends. You must be at your best when dealing with people who are important to you. This block, as well as most of the others, is self-explanatory, but that is the great part about the Pyramid. Anyone in any walk of life can understand that we should be our best and enjoy a challenge. The building blocks seem simple, but when put into action, they are amazing.

The Pyramid of Success is a wonderful tool that, as a whole, has taught me how to be a better person. But I have learned more than the Pyramid could ever teach, from the man who created it. Papa is truly an inspiration to me and to everyone who knows him.

Cori and Coach at her
high school graduation

THE PYRAMID

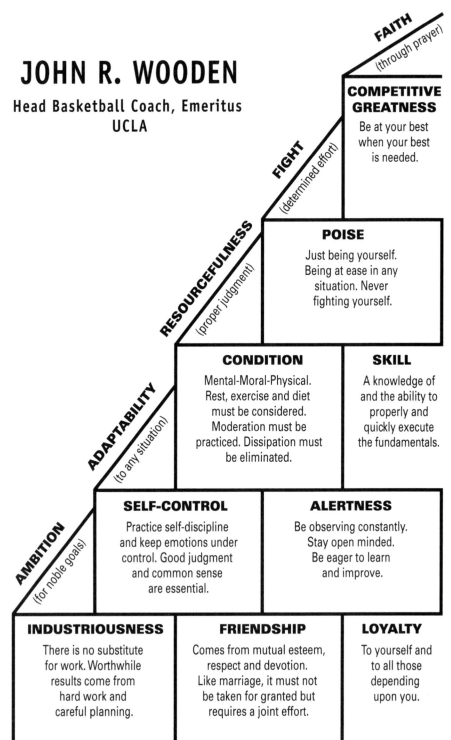

JOHN R. WOODEN

Head Basketball Coach, Emeritus
UCLA

FAITH (through prayer)

FIGHT (determined effort)

RESOURCEFULNESS (proper judgment)

ADAPTABILITY (to any situation)

AMBITION (for noble goals)

COMPETITIVE GREATNESS
Be at your best when your best is needed.

POISE
Just being yourself. Being at ease in any situation. Never fighting yourself.

CONDITION
Mental-Moral-Physical. Rest, exercise and diet must be considered. Moderation must be practiced. Dissipation must be eliminated.

SKILL
A knowledge of and the ability to properly and quickly execute the fundamentals.

SELF-CONTROL
Practice self-discipline and keep emotions under control. Good judgment and common sense are essential.

ALERTNESS
Be observing constantly. Stay open minded. Be eager to learn and improve.

INDUSTRIOUSNESS
There is no substitute for work. Worthwhile results come from hard work and careful planning.

FRIENDSHIP
Comes from mutual esteem, respect and devotion. Like marriage, it must not be taken for granted but requires a joint effort.

LOYALTY
To yourself and to all those depending upon you.

OF SUCCESS™

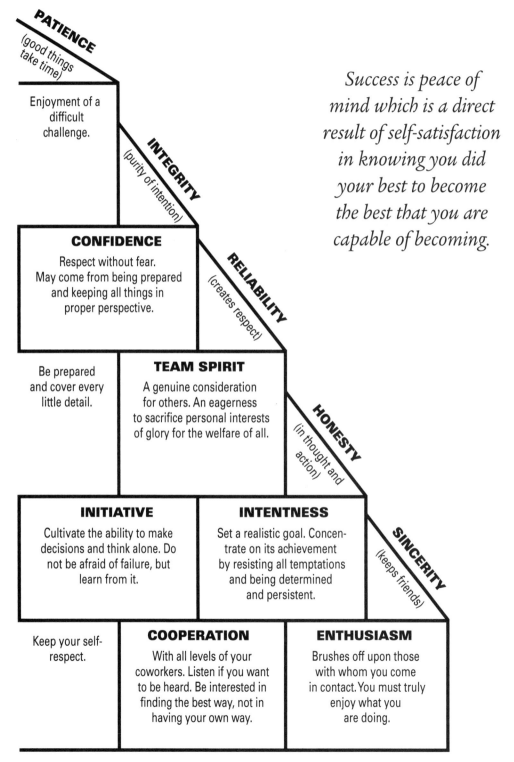

PATIENCE
(good things take time)

Enjoyment of a difficult challenge.

Success is peace of mind which is a direct result of self-satisfaction in knowing you did your best to become the best that you are capable of becoming.

INTEGRITY
(purity of intention)

CONFIDENCE
Respect without fear. May come from being prepared and keeping all things in proper perspective.

RELIABILITY
(creates respect)

Be prepared and cover every little detail.

TEAM SPIRIT
A genuine consideration for others. An eagerness to sacrifice personal interests of glory for the welfare of all.

HONESTY
(in thought and action)

INITIATIVE
Cultivate the ability to make decisions and think alone. Do not be afraid of failure, but learn from it.

INTENTNESS
Set a realistic goal. Concentrate on its achievement by resisting all temptations and being determined and persistent.

SINCERITY
(keeps friends)

Keep your self-respect.

COOPERATION
With all levels of your coworkers. Listen if you want to be heard. Be interested in finding the best way, not in having your own way.

ENTHUSIASM
Brushes off upon those with whom you come in contact. You must truly enjoy what you are doing.

Coach John Wooden of Westwood
A Messenger on Call
by William D. Naulls

Coach John Wooden of Westwood has a message for all.
Industriousness and *enthusiasm*, the cornerstones of his call.
Focused on *friendship* and *loyalty*, he stresses *cooperation*
    and mastery of *intentness* of *initiative* through *self-
    controlled* participation.
Not to forget *alertness* and *condition* in developing *team
    spirit's skill*
of maturing *competitive greatness, poise* and *confidence* to
    fulfill.
Inspired by *sincerity* of *ambition* and an honest desire to be
    "as He,"
men and women can achieve their best through responsible
    adaptability.
Reliability on the *resourcefulness* possessed in *integrity's* might
is the victory of the good *fight* of *faith*, through *patience's*
    insight.
So the message of life, of Coach Wooden's call—
    SUCCESS is a reward to anyone who gives his all.

INDUSTRIOUSNESS (HARD WORK)

*There is no substitute for work. Worthwhile results come
from hard work and careful planning.*

WOODEN

Industriousness has two components—work and planning. Let's start with work.

There is no substitute for hard work. Most people have a tendency to look for shortcuts or at least for the easiest way to complete any given task. If we only put out a minimum effort we might get by in some situations, but in the long run we won't fully develop the talents that lie within us.

I learned the importance of work on the farm where I was raised. My parents worked very hard and taught us to follow their example. There was time for play, but it always came after the chores were done. As a result, hard work became part of my nature.

As a basketball player, I wanted to be in the best possible physical condition. There was a time when I'd tell myself, *I'm going to be in better condition that anyone else.* As I grew older, my thinking changed to *I'm going to be in the best possible condition I can be.* I had learned that I only have control over myself.

I worked hard at playing basketball and I was considered a very aggressive player. I was knocked to the floor a lot because I would drive to the basket and I would also go after loose balls. A sports writer nicknamed me the Indiana rubber man. He said that I bounced back up like a rubber ball. I received that nickname as a result of someone else observing my hard work. However, playing hard is not the same as being overly aggressive. Too much aggression results in a loss of control, which produces mistakes. While I was aggressive, I always tried to be under control.

Off the court, I worked hard, too. In 1948, I became head basketball coach at UCLA. During my tenure in Westwood, I never took an extended break after the season was over. A couple of weeks after our last game, I would begin research on some aspect of the sport. I would talk with other coaches, read books and examine every angle. The season usually ended in March. My research would last for the entire off-season, from March until the beginning of the next school year, in the fall.

I have always wanted to be the best I can be. I still do, so I work at it. My knees and hips make it difficult to walk very far or stand very long, but I keep up with a busy speaking and traveling schedule. I continue to meet with individuals during the week. And I still answer every letter I receive.

I used to read more than I do now. My eyes are failing some. I don't remember quite as well as I once did; my memory is going, too. But I will continue to do the best I can with what I have. Although I don't know any other 94-year-olds who work as hard as I do, that is not the point. The only competition I have is with myself. Even at 94, I want to be the best I can be, and hard work is the only way to make this happen.

Good planning and hard work lead to prosperity, but hasty shortcuts lead to poverty (Proverbs 21:5).

CARTY

Coach Wooden not only worked hard, but he also spent much of his life teaching others to put out a maximum effort. That's hard work in itself. It's a hard lesson that few people ever learn.

Most people slack off when they think their lack of effort will go undetected. But there is someone who is always looking. God sees us every minute of every day and He wants us to work as if what we are doing is a gift to Him.

As the director of a Christian camp, I spent five years helping young people become the best they could be. The greatest challenge of the year was teaching summer staff members to apply Ephesians 6:7: "Work with enthusiasm, as though you were working for the Lord rather than for people."

Few tasks are as taxing as serving campers for nine weeks. The hours are long and the work is hard and thankless. The last three weeks separate the cream from the milk. Those who keep their commitments and give it their all willingly cover both for the slackers and for those who can't cut it and leave early. The staff members who endure learn that there is much more inside them than they ever imagined. They are the ones who are more apt to become all they are capable of becoming. They are the ones who are more likely to find success as Coach Wooden defines it. Working hard, digging deep and bringing out the good from within us are the keys.

The staff members who endured had dug deep within themselves for a few days; however, the trick is to commit to digging deep for a lifetime, like Coach has. The apostle Paul made such a commitment. Paul is a great example of a tireless, hard worker. He showed the trait both before he was a Christian and once he became a believer. In his pre-Christian days, he was known as Saul, the relentless persecutor of the Church.[1] As Paul, he endured great hardship to plant churches in many lands.[2] He even paid his own way, working as a tentmaker.

Paul reminded people:

Don't you remember, dear brothers and sisters, how hard we worked among you? Night and day we toiled to earn a living so that our expenses would not be a burden to anyone there as we preached God's Good News among you (1 Thessalonians 2:9).

Being an apostle was hard work, but Paul loved it. He didn't work for people or for himself; rather, he worked for God's glory.[3] When we follow Paul's example, it's easier to give our all. Recognizing hard work as a gift to the Lord is the cornerstone to becoming all we are capable of becoming.

YOUR TURN

■ **Today's reading:** Proverbs 13:4,11; 14:23; 22:29; 28:19; 31:13-27; Ephesians 6:7; 1 Corinthians 10:31

1. Coach took his path to excellence by choosing an aspect of the game and studying it thoroughly. Make a list of issues in your life that need some hard work. Choose one area and establish a plan to develop excellence. Who will you contact? What will you read? What will you do?

2. Jay writes about reaching beyond the perceived limits of our ability. In what area do you think you can push past your current limitations? How will you accomplish this?

❏ I commit myself to a lifestyle of hard work so that I can become all God created me to be.

Heavenly Father, help me to view the effort I give in every aspect of my life as a gift to You. Lord, teach me to work for You and not for people. I want to fulfill the plans You have for me—for Your glory. Thank You.

INDUSTRIOUSNESS (PLANNING)

*There is no substitute for work. Worthwhile results
come from hard work and careful planning.*

WOODEN

In *Inch and Miles*, I boiled down the concept of industriousness to
"work," but that book is for children and needed to be simple. Here
we need to expand industrious to include planning. Undirected dili-
gence isn't very efficient; therefore, an element of planning must go
into hard work. It is the combination of the two that results in
industriousness.

When I coached basketball at UCLA, I believed that if we were
going to succeed, we needed to be industrious. One way I accomplished this was with proper planning. I spent two hours with my
staff planning each practice. Each drill was calculated to the minute.
Every aspect of the session was choreographed, including where the
practice balls would be placed. I did not want any time lost by people running over to a misplaced-ball bin.

I think, for the most part, my strength as a teacher emerged from
planning and organization. By having practices carefully orchestrat-
ed, we were able to get more done in a shorter period of time.
Practice under some coaches runs for three hours. Mine lasted an
hour and a half to two hours. We didn't waste time.

For example, I didn't split the team into small groups, then talk
to each group one at a time as some coaches do, and I rarely stopped
practice to make a point. I didn't want the other players standing
around while I spoke to only a few. If there was a need to address an
individual or a group of players, I did it while the others watched or
during the flow of whatever drill we were conducting.

Early in my coaching career, I learned an important principle from legendary basketball coach John Bunn. In *Basketball Methods,* he wrote, "Don't take thirty minutes to say something you should say in thirty seconds."[1] Bunn was erudite, a great speaker and a brilliant man, but he didn't practice what he preached. He would expound way too long on details that didn't require that much explanation. I learned from his error and always kept the few team meetings I had short.

I was a stickler for time management almost from the beginning. With me, being on time was and still is vital. Nonetheless, in my early days of teaching, sometimes when things weren't going well, I kept my team longer. This was counterproductive. I learned that when players are tired physically they are usually tired mentally as well. It took me too long to learn that this does not lead to industrious.

I also discovered that if practice did not always end when it was supposed to end, players would hold back a little effort and energy. When I saw this happening, I became a stickler for stopping on time. Whether we practiced an hour and a half or two hours, my players knew exactly when we were going to stop and I stuck to it. They had no reason to hold anything back. As a result they worked harder during the scheduled time, and we got more done in a shorter amount of time.

If people are going to become all that they are capable of becoming, it is important that they work hard; but it is also important that they are *intentional* about the hard work. Planning places effort where effort is most needed. People who put these two components together have a firm cornerstone of industriousness upon which they can build toward success.

Good planning and hard work lead to prosperity, but hasty shortcuts lead to poverty (Proverbs 21:5).

CARTY

Coach had a plan for his team that enabled the players to be the best that they could be. Likewise, God has a plan for each of us that will enable us to be all that He created us to be. However, at first glance, God's idea of preparation is not so obvious.

God is sovereign and He has plans for each of us.[2] Such an arrangement seems simple enough until we consider that He also gives us free will and He expects us to make plans.

How are we to go about making plans? Proverbs provides practical instruction: "Commit your work to the LORD, and then your plans will succeed" (16:3). There, however, is a caveat: "You can make many plans, but the Lord's purpose will prevail" (Proverbs 19:21).

This is an old lesson. A long time ago, a group of people planned to build a monument to their own greatness. It was designed to reach into heaven and was to be called the Tower of Babel. Since the people were trying to worship themselves rather than God, God stopped the project and implemented another one. He scrambled the language of the people of that day and scattered them to the ends of the earth.[3]

Despite the paradoxes and cautions, our job appears to be dreaming up plans. In fact, God sometimes helps with the dreams. He gave Pharaoh a dream, then showed Joseph the interpretation, which involved the need for a plan. As a result, Joseph was given the responsibility to use seven years of plenty to gather and store food in order to get Egypt, and everyone around them who wanted to eat, through seven years of famine. Joseph's ability to plan and make provision for the bad years saved a nation and a people.[4]

A tough part about planning is waiting. Some people make their plans and ask God to bless them, then immediately start to act out the plan. Others show patience. They diligently prepare, but then they wait until God says go. Waiting upon God does not justify the avoidance of hard work. To the contrary, it takes proper planning to make hard work efficient and productive. Moreover, we should not only work hard at our jobs, but we must also be diligent in every area of life. We need to plan well and work hard at being a spouse, a parent, a friend, a shortstop on the church softball team, a volunteer at the local animal shelter and in every other role we take on.

Coach calls that industriousness, a cornerstone in the Pyramid of Success.

YOUR TURN

■ **Today's reading:** Psalm 33:11; Jeremiah 29:11; Psalm 40:5; Proverbs 16:3; Proverbs 19:21; Genesis 11:4-6; Luke 14:28; Genesis 41:46-57; Jeremiah 29:11; 1 Corinthians 15:58

1. Make a list of the activities of your week. Estimate the time spent on each activity. Does the time spent reflect the time you'd like to spend? If not, what are you going to do about it?

2. Establish a daily time for devotions and prayer. Set a consistent time each day and be specific about starting and ending times. Knowing that plans are sometimes interrupted, devise a backup plan for your time of reflection so you can meet that goal even when you encounter unforeseen elements.

❏ I commit myself to establishing and maintaining a time of reflection.

Lord God, thank You for the plans You have for me and that they are plans for welfare and not calamity. Guide me in making my plans an outward expression of Your plans. Show me the value of combining hard work with careful planning that I might be more efficient in furthering Your Kingdom. Thank You.

ENTHUSIASM

Brushes off upon those with whom you come in contact.
You must truly enjoy what you are doing.

WOODEN

I think we have to enjoy what we do if we are to succeed.

We almost have to force or drive ourselves to work hard if we are to reach our potential. If we don't enjoy what we do, we won't be able to push as hard as we need to push for as long as we need to push to achieve our best. However, if we do enjoy what we do, and if we're enthusiastic about it, we'll do it better and come closer to becoming the best we can be.

We're more productive when we do the tasks we like to do. For example, in retirement I don't *have* to do much of anything. Nonetheless, in some respects, I am busier than ever. The difference is that now I do what I choose to do rather than what I have to do. In most things, I am enthusiastic; therefore, I am willing. However, some tasks can still become drudgery—that's when I will lose my enthusiasm.

When I arrived at UCLA, I wondered what I had gotten myself into. Being from the Midwest, Southern California shocked me. Moreover, I'd seen the basketball players with whom I was going to work, and I didn't feel that they measured up to the players who I'd left in Indiana. Also, the conditions in the UCLA gymnasium were horrendous compared to what I had had. I admit that I was down until I decided to enthusiastically accept the challenge before me.

I had sunk into emotional doldrums because I had allowed circumstances over which I have no control to hurt the aspects of my life over which I did have control. I had gone against my own philosophy. It took too long for me to realize, but the time did come when I concluded that I had to make the most of what I had, instead of worrying about the things that I didn't have. I look back with regret, feeling that I failed the people who were under my supervision prior to my coming to that realization. However, it's important to accept our mistakes and learn from them. We cannot use them as excuses. I've tried to do that, too. It simply does not work.

We won our first national championship in that old gymnasium. Do you think we could have done that if my enthusiasm hadn't rubbed off on everyone in our program? I don't think so.

I'm convinced that regardless of task, leaders must be enthusiastic and really enjoy what they're doing if they expect those under their supervision to work near their respective levels of competency. With few exceptions, an unenthusiastic leader will keep those under his or her charge from achieving their collective best.

Enthusiasm can stimulate others. I've often used it, but in moderation. Extreme highs do not work. In fact, too much emotion can be counterproductive. Highs lead to lows—such swings of intensity result in instability. I wanted my players on an even keel so that their thinking wasn't adversely affected by emotion. Quiet enthusiasm got results. It exudes confidence and rubs off in wonderful ways.

Never be lazy in your work, but serve the Lord enthusiastically (Romans 12:11).

CARTY

Kareem Abdul-Jabbar was winding down his professional basketball career—or so he thought. Then along came Magic Johnson.

On opening night in 1979, Kareem hit a buzzer-beater to win the game. Johnson went bananas, slapping high fives and hugging everyone. Acting like someone who had just won a championship, Magic even bear-hugged Kareem. The stoic veteran asked the rookie to calm down. It would be a long season.

The next time the Lakers won, there Magic was with his high fives. Magic's enthusiasm was contagious and his teammates caught it. James Worthy ran like a deer. Michael Cooper hit shots from long range. Kareem became a kid again. Thus, what was called "Show-time" was born.

Apollos was enthusiastic, too. He was rubbing people the right way with his fervor, but there was a problem. He didn't know the whole story. Apollos understood and taught Old Testament Scriptures, theology and prophecy—he even taught accurately about Jesus, but he only went as far as John's Baptism. His enthusiasm was rubbing off, but he wasn't getting people excited about the right thing.

When Apollos arrived in Ephesus, the local Bible study leaders, a godly couple named Priscilla and Aquila, heard his bold, enthusiastic preaching and saw a diamond in the rough. They took Apollos aside and explained things to him more accurately. Apollos took good notes. When he went on to Achaia, "He refuted all the Jews with powerful arguments in public debate. Using the Scriptures, he explained to them, 'The Messiah you are looking for is Jesus'" (Acts 18:28).

Apollos preached with enthusiasm. It was his passion for the Word that set him apart and his humility that kept him straight. When people started bragging about and following certain mentors instead of Christ, Apollos would have nothing to do with it. Paul and he were opposed to creating followers of Apollos or followers of Paul.[1] Instead, they wanted to produce enthusiastic followers of Christ.

Biblical enthusiasm means to boil in the spirit, to commit with your whole heart and to be zealous and passionate. God wants us to be that way about Him and His Son, and He wants us to be that way about becoming all that He designed us to be. However, enthusiasm alone won't carry us very far for very long. Like Apollos, we need knowledge to get it right.

Enthusiasm is a cornerstone in the Pyramid of Success, but when it comes to faith, it must be coupled with knowledge.

YOUR TURN

- **Today's reading:** Psalm 42:1-2; Ecclesiastes 12:1; Romans 12:11; Acts 18:24-28; 1 Corinthians 1:12; 3:4-6; 4:6; 22; Galatians 6:9; Revelation 2:4

1. Out of all the tasks that you do, list the three that you enjoy the most and the three that you enjoy the least.

2. Which of your responsibilities do you enjoy the least? Are these expectations from others or duties you have created for yourself? How can you develop enthusiasm to complete these less-than-enjoyable tasks, particularly the ones over which you have no control?

❑ I commit myself to a lifestyle of enthusiasm.

Almighty God of Excitement and Passion, I want to serve You with my whole heart and every fiber of my being. Give me a passion for Your Son that will rub off on all You place in my path and the knowledge and understanding to be firm in my faith. Father, I want to become all that I can become as Your enthusiastic representative. May it be so.

ENTHUSIASM

FRIENDSHIP

Comes from mutual esteem, respect and devotion.
Like marriage, it must not be taken for granted
but requires a joint effort.

WOODEN

The three blocks I chose to put between the cornerstones are the "people blocks" of "friendship," "loyalty" and "cooperation." People make us better. It is easier to reach our potential when we learn the value of including others in our quest. We can accomplish so much more when we work with others.

If we are going to successfully work with others, it is vital to know the role of friendship. Friendship comes from mutual esteem and devotion. God created us to be interdependent. We were not designed to go through life alone. We become so much more when we come alongside others—and we make them better, too. One of my former players at UCLA, Swen Nater, captured this concept in a poem he wrote:

Friendship
If someone does a kindly deed
For someone else who had a need,
Although a million he may lend,
That person still is not a friend.

If someone sees your heavy load
And bears your burden down the road
Though hills and mountains you ascend,
That person still is not a friend.

Friendship is a fine, fine art
Where each has helped the other's heart

And loyalty has helped both know,
We make it build and shape and grow.

There's shared respect, just like a team.
Devotion, love, regard, esteem
It will take time, but on the course
A friendship pulls a powerful course

A force so strong that when it's done,
It turns the two into a one
And one plus one's no longer true,
When two become much more than two.[1]

Friendship is doing for others while they are doing for you. It's called ministry when all of the doing goes in one direction. Friendship goes both ways. Friendship is like a good marriage—it's based on mutual concern. Friends help each other; they don't use each other.

Would you rather be successful in your eyes or in the eyes of others? If you said, "Others," your reputation may be fine, but your character is suspect. Your reputation is what you're perceived to be. Your character is what you really are. They can be different. I've often said that we should be more concerned about our character than our reputation. I don't think a good reputation is worth much if you have faulty character and don't have peace within yourself. If you use your friends to advance a personal agenda, you'll never be at peace.

Make friends and maintain friendships. Friends help to complete us, and we'll be better for having taken them along on our journey to becoming all we are capable of becoming.

A person standing alone can be attacked and defeated, but two can stand back-to-back and conquer. Three are even better, for a triple-braided cord is not easily broken (Ecclesiastes 4:12).

43

CARTY

The Bible contains much about friendship. Examples and lessons abound. Ruth and her mother-in-law were tight.[2] David and Jonathan were as close as two people can get.[3] Job's friends came to console him when he lost everything.[4] And the Bible lists nearly 90 people who were connected to the apostle Paul, many of whom he called dear friends.

In Daniel, we read about three Jewish men who were friends. Shadrach, Meshach and Abednego (just call them My Shack, Your Shack and A Bungalow) were so close that they took the heat and walked together in obedience. They even faced death together. They had a friendship that included accountability. While there are many aspects to being accountable as friends, we see in these three the results of such a commitment when it is put to a test.

King Nebuchadnezzar ordered everyone in his kingdom to worship his statue. The dilemma for Shadrach, Meshach and Abednego was that they only worshiped the one true God; therefore, they refused to bow down to Nebuchadnezzar's statue. As a result, Nebuchadnezzar had them thrown into a fiery furnace. As the king watched, nothing happened. The trio was as cool as the other side of the pillow. Their hair wasn't singed, their clothes hadn't burned, and they didn't even smell of smoke.[5] What the king saw changed his life and he too became a believer in the one true God.

What would have happened if the three hadn't had each other? Individually, would they have caved in to save their respective skins? Who knows? But we do know that collectively they were strong. They formed a triple-braided cord that could not easily be broken. That's the value of friends who are accountable to each other.

Do you have friends to whom you are accountable? If not, I recommend that you find two or three friends of your gender, agree to meet regularly and ask each other the hard questions about lust, greed, anger, revenge and covetousness. Hold each other accountable for answers and behavior. Help your friends walk straight lines and push them toward becoming all that they are all capable of becoming. Allow them to do the same for you. It is what good friends ought to do.

YOUR TURN

■ **Today's reading:** Daniel 3:3—4:3; Proverbs 17:17; 18:24; Ecclesiastes 4:12; 1 Corinthians 13:4-7; John 15:13; Philippians 2:3

1. Based on Coach's definition of friendship, make a list of the people in your life who would qualify as your friends.

2. Look at your list of friends. Who on that list do you trust the most? How could you go about establishing accountability with that person or persons?

❏ I commit myself to being accountable.

Dear Author of Friendship, I thank You that I can have You as a friend through Jesus Christ my Lord. Please send a few good friends my way so that I can be part of a three-strand cord of strength and bring more glory to Your Name. Use me to help them and them to help me faithfully walk with You. Thank You.

COOPERATION

With all levels of your coworkers. Listen if you want to be heard. Be interested in finding the best way, not in having your own way.

WOODEN

Cooperation is working with others for the benefit of all. It is not sacrificing for someone else's benefit. If what you are doing doesn't help everyone involved, then it is something other than cooperation, perhaps you would call it ministry, service or selfishness.

Some individuals, such as writers and scientists, often work alone and accomplish much. But in my opinion, those who primarily work alone will never become all they could become if they were working with others. Working with others makes us much more than we could ever become alone.

Because it was such a formative observation in my youth, I have often told the following story: When I was a young boy, I was at a gravel pit with my father and a young man. They had a team of horses and were attempting to pull a load up a steep road. The young man driving the horses was loud and abusive. In response, the animals were hyper and agitated. They worked against each other and, as a result, couldn't pull the load. With a gentle voice and a gentler touch, my dad calmed the horses and walked them forward with the load. When the horses cooperated, they could do much more than when they didn't work together.

I learned two important lessons that day: (1) Gentleness is a better method of getting cooperation than harshness is; (2) A team can accomplish much more when it works together than individuals can when they work alone. I tried to apply both principles when I was a teacher/coach. I believe most of my teams demonstrated the effectiveness of the applications.

My first national championship team (1964) probably operated as a team as much as any team I have ever seen. I'll never forget the conversation between coaches before our final game against Duke. The Blue Devils had two players who stood 6-foot-10. We didn't have anyone over 6-foot-5. The general consensus was that UCLA was a fine little team, but Duke was a fine big team. However, a European coach observed, "UCLA will win because they are a team." I considered that a very nice compliment.

Running our press was the ultimate test of the cooperative spirit. Every player had to cover for somebody else, and they had to trust each other to do that. When applying our press, the team came to expect to make at least two runs each game during which we would score six to eight points in a row. I believe the players collectively looked for whoever was able to help the team most on any given night, rather than always looking to one individual. The abilities of the players served the team, as opposed to the players being used to serve an individual. That's cooperation.

Ironically, my players that year weren't that close off the floor. They certainly varied in how much they liked one another. After a game or practice they all went their separate ways, but they were completely loyal to each other on the court. No one tried to be a star. They were each nonassuming and accomplished far more than anyone expected.

Two people can accomplish more than twice as much as one; they get a better return for their labor (Ecclesiastes 4:9).

CARTY

Like John Wooden's first championship team, God's first worship team was based on cooperation. King David was the coach.

Before God had Solomon build the Temple, the children of God had the tabernacle. It was a plain, movable tent. God had described the items He wanted to be used in worship, but He waited for Coach

David's era to put His best worship team together.

Early in David's anointing, he and Samuel the prophet drew up plans for a worship team. Many years later, after Samuel had died and Saul had been killed, it was time for David to enact the plan. David organized teams and assigned seven-day-long shifts.

There were 212 gatekeepers who rotated duties. Their responsibilities were to open the doors every morning and shut them at night, keep away anyone who wasn't qualified to worship, and direct traffic. Other workers took care of the plates, vessels and utensils. Separate teams prepared wine, oil and fine flour for offerings. Other groups oversaw meat offerings, grain offerings and show bread. And shifts of singers sang songs of praise and worship around the clock so that the earthly temple would be a symbol of the heavenly temple where praise goes up 24/7.[1] The roles of the people on the worship team were carefully defined, and the members functioned as a well-coordinated unit.

Just as David and Samuel were assigned to develop the job descriptions for the Old Testament worship team, Paul and Peter were given the responsibility to stimulate the use of spiritual gifts among the team of believers in the New Testament Church. Paul wrote:

> Just as our bodies have many parts and each part has a special function, so it is with Christ's body. We are all parts of his one body, and each of us has different work to do. And since we are all one body in Christ, we belong to each other, and each of us needs all the others (Romans 12:4-5).

In other words, let's cooperate as we use our spiritual gifts.

More than 20 gifts are noted in the gifts Scriptures.[2] However, most Bible scholars do not think the list is exhaustive. Every believer is given at least one spiritual gift,[3] and probably more.

A problem occurs when a member of the Body of Christ doesn't use his or her gifts.[4] That stifles cooperation, and the team suffers.

Just as the whole body hurts when an organ doesn't function, so it is when a member of the Body of Christ chooses not to participate.

Just as we need friends for accountability, we also need partners to maximize our spiritual potential. Corporate efforts will add to the Body of Christ in ways well beyond what could ever be accomplished individually.

YOUR TURN

■ **Today's reading:** 1 Chronicles 9:22-34; Psalm 84:10; Ecclesiastes 4:9,12; Revelation 4:8; Romans 12:3-8; Ephesians 4:7-16; 1 Corinthians 12:1-11; 1 Peter 4:10; 1 Thessalonians 5:19

1. List all contexts where you find yourself in a cooperative group.

2. Where, in your experience, are you working alone and could benefit from the cooperation of a companion or group? What steps will you take to develop a team in one of these areas?

❏ I commit myself to developing a team spirit in all I do.

Dear Lord God, You are the Author of interdependency. You gave us a need for each other. Give me a willingness to cooperate with my brothers and sisters in Christ. Maximize our spiritual potential so as to bring greater glory to Your name. Thank You.

LOYALTY

To yourself and to all those depending upon you. Keep your self-respect.

WOODEN

When I was playing basketball at Purdue University, I wore my hair rather short and close-cropped. Some youngsters who followed our team wanted to wear their hair the same way. When they went to the barbershop they would say, "I want to get a Putnamville bob."

The origin of that name comes from the reformatory that is located in Putnamville, Indiana. The boys in that institution had to wear their hair buzzed, or bobbed off. My haircut was known as the Putnamville bob and many boys who also wore it that way were loyal fans.

Loyalty, however, is more than emulating someone's looks. That is attachment or identification, but the depth of the word "loyalty" comes into play when we add concepts such as devotion, duty, faithfulness and commitment. It's interesting that these virtues can be given to people, teams, organizations, governments, countries, ideals, rulers, religions and God.

Loyalty is the foundational quality that gets us through hard times. Will we compromise our integrity when temptation is great? Or will we remain loyal to our beliefs and core values?

I have often cautioned people that we can become great in the eyes of others, but we'll never become successful when we compromise our character and show disloyalty toward friends or teammates. The reverse is also true: No individual or team will become great without loyalty.

In basketball, we want to know if we can count on our teammates. When we know that they will be there to support us in tight spots, we are more likely to go the extra mile when they too need help. That combination makes each of us better. Loyalty is the force that forges individuals into a team.[1] It's the component that moves teams toward great achievements. That's why, as a coach, I always stressed it.

When I came to UCLA, the situation was not as I expected; but I had a three-year contract, so I stayed. I would have compromised my word by leaving, and my word is a core value.

I understand that today many employers aren't loyal to their employees, and a growing number of employees aren't loyal to their employers; but I'm what is called "old school"—I believe in the value of loyalty. I do not have a problem with an NBA player requesting a contract extension or a renegotiation, but to threaten to not give his best if his contract isn't changed (as has happened) compromises his integrity. It's not right. There is something wrong when your loyalty is always available to the highest bidder.

Another old-school quality that I have chosen to maintain is the fact that I am a one-woman man. Nellie and I were married for 53 years. I've never been with another woman. When she died two decades ago, I decided to remain loyal. To honor her, on the twenty-first day of each month I wrote her a letter. I still write on special occasions. I put the letter on her pillow for a night and then put it away with the other letters I've written. I was loyal to her in life, and I will remain loyal to her memory until we are forever together again.

So then, brethren, stand firm and hold to the traditions which you were taught, whether by word of mouth or by letter from us (2 Thessalonians 2:15, *NASB*).

CARTY

Check out 1 Chronicles 11:10-12,37. The story is about real-life action heroes. It's okay to skim through the list of names, but look at the stories. Jashobeam killed 300 men at one time with just a spear,[2] and some guys broke through the Philistine lines just to get

LOYALTY

David a drink. What David did with the water will amaze you, and you'll gain a new appreciation of what loyalty really means.

David was loyal to his men and his men were so loyal to him that they made him their king. David's men were also loyal to each other. Uriah the Hittite was on the front lines fighting the Ammonites. When he was the only one called home, he was so loyal to his fellow fighters that he refused the pleasures his wife and home had to offer. If his mates couldn't enjoy their homes, he refused to enjoy his. His reasoning came from his loyalty to God and to his comrades in arms.

> Uriah replied, "The Ark and the armies of Israel and Judah are living in tents, and Joab and his officers are camping in the open fields. How could I go home to wine and dine and sleep with my wife? I swear that I will never be guilty of acting like that" (2 Samuel 11:11).

In an earlier Old Testament scene, when it came time to possess the land, the tribes of Reuben, Gad and half of the tribe of Manasseh preferred the ground east of the Jordan River, but they demonstrated their loyalty by assisting their brothers in securing their land to the west. It wasn't until all the land had been conquered that they settled onto their own land. Many people gave their lives to fulfill their responsibilities to their kin, but they kept their promise: "We will not return to our homes until all the people of Israel have received their inheritance of land" (Numbers 32:18). They kept their word—that's called loyalty.

God wants us to be like David's men. He wants us to make Him King in our lives. Like Uriah was, God wants us to be passionately loyal to His team of believers. He wants our loyalty to the Father to pass the test of the tribes of Reuben, Gad and Manasseh. For the sake of God and the advancement of His Kingdom, would you put your life on the line if called or required to do so? The way events have been unfolding in our world, that time may be near. In fact, in some nations, such as North Korea, our persecuted brothers and sisters already face this reality.

God definitely demands old-school loyalty—of us and of Himself.[3] In fact, our Heavenly Father thinks it's cool to be old school.

YOUR TURN

■ **Today's reading:** 1 Chronicles 11:10—12:37; 2 Samuel 11:2-13; Numbers 32:6-18; Hebrews 13:8; James 1:17; 2 Thessalonians 2:13-15

1. Recount times when you made a commitment to be loyal to someone and it proved costly. Recall one time when you depended on someone to be loyal to you and he or she failed. Describe the emotions you felt at that time and afterward regarding that incident and that person.

2. Based on your experience of being let down by someone, how would you describe the nature of God's forgiveness and His response to our sin?

❑ I commit myself to a lifestyle of being loyal to my family, my colleagues, my friends, my spouse and those to whom I have given my word.

> *Oh, God, I want You and You alone to be my God. I offer You everything I have, including my devotion and loyalty. May I faithfully carry out my responsibilities in Your Kingdom and my responsibilities to all believers. With all my heart, I want my loyalty to pass the tests and temptations that will be coming my way. Give me strength to stand firm. Thank You.*

SELF-CONTROL

Practice self-discipline and keep emotions under control.
Good judgment and common sense are essential.

WOODEN

Self-control is the ability to discipline ourselves and keep our emotions under control. To become our best, good judgment and common sense are essential. No matter the task—whether physical or mental—if our emotions take over, we're not going to execute near our personal level of competency, because both judgment and common sense will be impaired. When our emotions dominate our actions, we make mistakes.

Let's apply this principle to hitting a golf ball. If we swing with a lot of emotion, the ball will be even further out to the right or left than it would be if we swung with self-control. Unless we're a pro, rarely will an emotional swing go down the middle, and never will it go down the middle with enough consistency to make us successful golfers.

A lack of self-control not only hinders individual achievement, but it also inhibits team accomplishment. Let's look at how this tenet works when disciplining someone we supervise. If emotion takes over, chances are we're going to antagonize that person. In my opinion, it's difficult to get productive, positive results under these circumstances. We must remember why we discipline. We do it to help, to prevent, to correct, and to improve, but not to punish.

I don't believe that punishment can consistently serve a productive purpose. We cannot give it or receive it and consistently be at our best. There have been many coaches who antagonize their players and appear to have been successful as far as their reputation is concerned; but I maintain that they could have been better as coaches and could have had better teams if they hadn't been punitive along the way.

In my senior year in high school, we were defeated in the Indiana state championship by one point. We lost the game when a player on the other team made a two-handed underhand heave from back of center court. I think I was the only player on my team who didn't cry. I had tried hard. I was at peace with myself. I felt badly, but I didn't have any reason to hang my head.

To this day, I honestly feel that every one of my ten national championship teams demonstrated more self-control than any other team I've ever seen. In every one of those championship games, when we had the game won, during a timeout I directed the players: "Now, don't make fools out of yourselves. Let's let the alumni and the fans do that. I know you want to get the nets and I know you feel good, and that's fine, but let's have no excessive exultation." I think all of my championship teams won with class and I'm proud of that.

> Knowing God leads to self-control. Self-control leads to patient endurance, and patient endurance leads to godliness (2 Peter 5:6).

CARTY

Coach Wooden would have been proud of Joseph. The lad had class and self-control. The cream always rises to the top, and Joseph was pure cream. The Lord was with him.[1] Having been sold into slavery, he moved up to become the number one honcho in Potiphar's house.

Potiphar was the captain of pharaoh's personal bodyguards, and Joseph was in charge of Potiphar's household and all of his businesses. All Potiphar had to think about was what he wanted to eat.[2] It was a sweet deal until the boss's wife started feeling frisky.

The Bible refers to Joseph as being handsome and well built.[3] Potiphar's wife noticed. She must have been a bored, rich, desperate housewife looking for a boy-toy. One day she invited Joseph into her bedroom.

SELF-CONTROL

What red-blooded young man wouldn't like to see himself as a chick magnet? Joseph was surely tempted, but he exercised self-control and chose to stay pure. Every day Potiphar's wife attempted to ensnare him and every day he resisted, until one day she grabbed him and held on. He had to slip out of his coat to get away.

Since Potiphar's wife couldn't have Joseph she decided to trash him—she claimed that he tried to rape her. Potiphar must have known his wife had wandering eyes. Instead of killing Joseph, Potiphar threw him in jail.

Joseph had self-control. He didn't let sexual inducement overcome him, and he didn't throw an emotional fit at God when he lost everything and landed in jail. Joseph never allowed his judgment to be clouded or his common sense to be compromised. Instead, he let the cream rise to the top and started running the prison. Because Joseph displayed self-control and faithfulness in reflecting his Heavenly Father's glory, God blessed him. Ultimately Joseph became pharaoh's right-hand man and second in control of Egypt.

Our job is to be like Joseph and be a mirror that reflects God's glory. The problem is that sin clouds our mirror, and each time we sin the mirror gets cloudier and God's reflection grows dimmer.

We can never be successful in the strictest of terms because we have all sinned by coming short of God's standard.[4] This means that sin has already decreased our potential. We can't be what we once could have been, but we can become all we are now capable of becoming. This means that we can still be successful. Achievement takes self-control to overcome temptation and prevent the further diminishment of our capacity to reflect God's glory.

If you know Jesus, then your Heavenly Father is proud of you and you'll spend eternity in heaven. However, your place in heaven will be determined by your reflection of His Son. Live with self-control and don't sin, so you can reflect to the max every day of your life.

YOUR TURN

■ **Today's reading:** Genesis 39:1-20; Romans 3:21-30; Galatians 5:16-24; James 3:1-12; 2 Peter 1:5-11

1. What areas of your life present the greatest difficulty in gaining and maintaining self-control?

2. Describe two or three encounters in which you have seen emotions hinder clear thinking.

❑ I commit myself to living a balanced life with greater self-control and sounder judgment.

Oh, God of Eternal Glory, I want all the days of my life to reflect the Glory of my Lord Jesus Christ. Help me to overcome temptation so that I might be all I am capable of becoming in honoring Your Holy Name. Thank You.

ALERTNESS

Be observing constantly. Stay open minded. Be eager to learn and improve.

WOODEN

We must be alert. We can do that by observing what is going on around us. Except for what we have garnered through personal experience, none of us knows anything that we didn't learn from somebody else. Whatever the lesson, we saw somebody do it, we read about it or we heard about it.

Abraham Lincoln is my favorite American hero. President Lincoln could always say so much with just a few words. My father often reminded me that Lincoln had said that he had never met a person from whom he did not learn something, although most of the time it was something not to do. There is a lot of truth in that; but the point is that Lincoln was always observing, alert to what was going on around him, and he was constantly learning.

When we aren't alert we miss opportunities to improve ourselves. If we remain attentive, not only can we improve ourselves, but we can also learn not to repeat the errors of others. We should always watch for circumstances or situations that can help or harm us and be eager to learn from our encounters.

Each of us has a huge capacity to learn and to achieve. Being ever alert makes the task of becoming all we are capable of becoming so much easier. I'm 94. My memory is not nearly as good as it once was. In fact, it's harder for me to read than it once was, but I am determined to keep learning. I am still inquisitive.

I suppose it's the measure of inquisitiveness in areas of interest that makes some people more alert than others. One of the most alert and inquisitive players I ever had under my supervision went on to be a great coach.

Denny Crum was a good player at UCLA, but he wasn't great.

Few remember him for his on-court abilities; but from his first day on the team, Denny wanted to know the reasoning behind every drill: "Why are we doing this?" "Why are you using this amount of time for it?" "Why do you place this drill at this particular point in practice?"

Denny Crum was born to coach. He was alert to everything about the game, and as a result he became one of the finest in his profession. As a result of his great success at the helm of the Louisville program, he was inducted into the Basketball Hall of Fame.

So many people have tunnel vision. They narrow their awareness. I wanted my players to always be searching, especially for truth. I wanted them to know what they believed and be able to defend it. Truth will always stand the test of scrutiny.

I'm not a relativist. I don't think we are supposed to find our own truth. That's playing God. I believe in absolute truth and absolute sin and the Bible is my standard for determining those absolutes. With that in mind, I believe that an inquisitive person is more apt to discover truth than someone with a closed mind. That's why alertness is a building block in the Pyramid of Success.

So let's not sleepwalk through life like those others. Let's keep our eyes open and be smart (1 Thessalonians 5:6, *THE MESSAGE*).

CARTY

The Israelites weren't always alert. There was a time when they closed their minds to God, turned their heads and rode a sin cycle. Someone on a sin cycle endures the consequences, repents of the sin, enjoys life for a while, forgets about God, sins again, endures, repents, enjoys, forgets, sins some more, and so on. When the Israelites fell into this trap, to get their attention God gave them over

ALERTNESS

to the Midianites. When they finally repented, God called upon Gideon.

Gideon's story includes the tearing down of an idol, two tests involving a fleece, the selection of the army, and a battle. Let's focus on the selection of Gideon's men, because God wanted only those who were alert.

God's plan called for Gideon and only three hundred of the most alert men in the camp to go up against the enemy's army. Gideon's opponent was not specifically numbered, but was said to be as numerous as locusts.[1] In other words, there probably were tens of thousands of enemy warriors! In today's vernacular, Gideon would have said, "No worries." When God is with you, it doesn't matter who or how many rise up against you.

Gideon assembled 32,000 farmers for the battle. That was way too many under God's strategy. God didn't want the people to take credit for the victory. To decrease the number, those who feared fighting were told to go home. Twenty-two thousand men decided they had back and stomach trouble (a yellow stripe and no guts) and departed; 10,000 men remained. That was still too many. God told Gideon to take his troops to the river and watch them drink. Those who bent down, took their eyes away from their surroundings, and drank like dogs were dismissed. Only 300 men passed the test. They lowered themselves to one knee, kept their heads up, kept their eyes peeled, stayed alert and used one hand to scoop water to their mouth. God chose the men who remained alert at all times.

What's the big deal about staying alert? God warned us, "Keep a cool head. Stay alert. The Devil is poised to pounce, and would like nothing better than to catch you napping" (1 Peter 5:8, *THE MESSAGE*). Another translation calls our enemy a roaring lion ready to devour us.[2]

God has given us a scouting report on our adversary. Satan is the father of lies. Whenever he speaks it's not the truth. He hates God and he wants our souls. If he can't have our souls, he at least wants us on a sin cycle. Sin keeps us from being alert to God's voice.

If you have been riding a sin cycle, perhaps it's time to stop what you've been doing, ask forgiveness through Jesus Christ, put on the whole armor of God[3] and stand firm. Once you've taken these steps, the keys to moving forward in God are staying alert, remaining watchful and filtering everything through His Holy Word.

YOUR TURN

■ **Today's reading:** Judges 6:1—7:23; 1 Corinthians 16:13; Ephesians 6:10-20; Colossians 4:2; 1 Thessalonians 5:6; 1 Peter 5:8

1. Are you riding a sin cycle? If you are, of what sins do you need to repent?

2. When is the last time you were aware of God's direction in your life? Would you like to know that He is leading you more frequently?

❏ I commit myself to continue listening to and learning about God and His plan for my life.

> *Holy God of Truth and Life, forgive me for the cycles of*
> *sin that I've allowed in my life. I haven't always been alert to*
> *Your leading. I repent. Please guard my heart, ears and eyes from*
> *the lies of our adversary. Help me to always be on guard, ever*
> *watchful and always alert to his schemes. I want to stand against*
> *him and I want to stand firm for You. May it be so.*

ALERTNESS

INITIATIVE

Cultivate the ability to make decisions and think alone.
Do not be afraid of failure, but learn from it.

WOODEN

Initiative is having the courage to make decisions and take action. People with initiative will act when action is needed.

People with initiative use all the information that they've previously acquired in regards to any particular situation, and they act with self-control. People with initiative move forward without fear of failure, even though they might make mistakes or fail.

If we allow the fear of failure to keep us from acting, we will never be a success or reach our full potential. Let's face it, we're all imperfect and we're going to fall short on occasion; but we must learn from failure, and that will enable us to avoid repeating our mistakes. Through adversity, we learn, grow stronger and become better people. When pondering this principle, I think of a poem I once memorized:

> When I look back, it seems to me,
> All the grief that had to be,
> Left me when the pain was O'er,
> Stronger than I was before.[1]

My college coach once said, "The team that makes the most mistakes will probably outscore the other one." What he meant is that doers make mistakes, but if we aren't doing anything we're making the greatest mistake of all. We must not fail to act when action is needed. We cannot be afraid. We must act anyhow, knowing that at times, we will fail.

There were times when I wasn't happy with practices because we seemed to be afraid to make a mistake. I wanted my players to be active. I wanted them to take initiative. I didn't want them worrying about mistakes, as long as they didn't repeat the same ones over and over (see Ralph Drollinger's essay in the appendix). I wanted them to learn from their mistakes. I didn't like conservative practices. I expected a certain number of turnovers in our scrimmages, but I wanted the right kind. Careless mistakes aren't the right kind.

Mistakes made while expanding boundaries are what I wanted. If we weren't making mistakes, we weren't far enough out on the edge. If we weren't pushing against the walls of our capabilities, we weren't practicing correctly. The time to cut down on turnovers is during games, although we should try to avoid them during practice, too.

When the game was tight, I wanted the person taking the last shot to be surprised if he missed. When we needed a basket badly, the player who wanted the ball was the one I wanted to have it. For example, in my next to the last game as a teacher, we were two points behind Louisville with only a few seconds to go. We set up a play for Richard Washington. Afterward a reporter asked, "Why did you pick Washington?" I replied, "Because he's not afraid to make a mistake. He thinks he's a pretty good shooter—and he is—but if he misses he'll think, *Well, you can't make them all.* He won't be devastated. Therefore, he's harnessed his fear. The others might be thinking, *I've got to make it.* If that's their thinking, they'll be fearful about missing. I didn't want that. I went with Richard."

He prayed more fervently, and he was in such agony of spirit that his sweat fell to the ground like great drops of blood (Luke 22:44).

CARTY

We all experience fear, anxiousness and other intense feelings. How we handle these emotions usually defines whether we become a hero or a coward—and there is a fine line between the two. Certain emotions can paralyze us and thus threaten to prevent us from becoming all we are capable of becoming. When this happens we must work through the particular feeling before we can reach success.

Intense feelings can even manifest in our bodies. For example, the famous NBA basketball player Bill Russell often got so nervous before games that he vomited. Moreover, it is commonplace for athletes to get diarrhea before sporting events. Fear, angst and apprehension can even make a person sweat blood. Jesus knew this.

The Messiah and His closest followers were in the Upper Room at the Last Supper. Jesus' spirit was troubled.[2] Since He was sinless, whatever emotion He felt wasn't anxiousness in the sense of the biblical admonition to "be anxious for nothing."[3] Instead, it was a strong feeling, and it would grow much more intense.

From the Upper Room, Jesus went to the Garden of Gethsemane to pray. The feeling intensified. Some Bible translations use words such as "troubled," "agony" and "anguish" in place of the Greek word that literally means "a contest involving great fear."[4] Jesus had the jitters.

As graphic as Mel Gibson's version of The Passion of the Christ was, he intentionally held back. Jesus' face would have been unrecognizable and most likely His ribs and backbone would have been exposed. That's what occurred when Roman soldiers scourged a man. However, the physical pain Jesus would endure was not His greatest concern.

The biggest issue He faced was being apart from the Father. Minimally, that's what hell is: complete and total separation from God. Disconnected from His Father, Jesus was uneasy. Who wouldn't be? For 12 hours, He would be beaten. He would take on the weight of the sin of humanity for eternity, and he would visit hell. How did Jesus prepare for the suffering? He fortified Himself with prayer.

The fact that Jesus sweated blood while He was praying is indicative of the lengths to which He had to go to if He was to overcome fear.[5] This wasn't a now-I-lay-me-down-to-sleep kind of prayer. Jesus agonized. It was literally a fearful contest between His flesh, satanic temptation and the Father's will.

The battle is summed up in Matthew 26:39:

> He went on a little farther and fell face down on the ground, praying, "My Father! If it is possible, let this cup of suffering be taken away from me. Yet I want your will, not mine."

In the flesh, Jesus didn't want to go through the suffering; but in His heart He wanted to do the Father's will more than His own. Jesus' greater desire overcame the paralysis of fear and initiated the greatest act of love the world has ever seen. On the cross, He became our greatest hero.

YOUR TURN

■ **Today's reading:** Luke 22:39-46; Matthew 26:36-45; John 13:21-30; Philippians 4:4-9

1. When was the last time that you attempted something new and it didn't work out? How did failure affect you?

2. Describe an event in your life when fear was present, but you did what you needed to do anyway.

❑ I commit to boldly press the boundaries of my life to reach my greatest potential.

Heavenly Father, help me to overcome the fears of life and look more like Your Son. Give me the courage to make decisions and take the actions that will represent Him and You well. Give me boldness for Jesus Christ. Thank You.

INTENTNESS

Set a realistic goal. Concentrate on its achievement by resisting all temptations and being determined and persistent.

WOODEN

I could have called this building block determination or perseverance. I suppose persistence or even tenacity would have been adequate. But intentness embraces all of those words and more, and it best states the final block on the second tier of the Pyramid of Success.

Intentness is the ability to resist temptation and to avoid rabbit trails of distraction. An intent person will stay the course and go the distance. He or she will concentrate on objectives with determination, stamina and resolve. Intentness is the quality that won't permit us to quit, even when our goal is going to take a while to accomplish.

Our society has been permeated by a mind-set of immediate gratification. Simply put, people are impatient. They want too much too soon. They have lost sight of an overarching truth: In life, worthwhile accomplishments and acquisitions take time. Usually the better the reward, the more time it takes to acquire it. Intentness gives us the doggedness to hang in there and overcome impatience. Intentness is patience with action. It's not wanting and waiting; rather, it's being able to wait while we act out a specific plan.

I believe in setting goals, but goals should be realistic, not idealistic or simplistic. Idealistic goals become counterproductive. When goals are set unrealistically high, it soon becomes apparent that they are not going to be met. This stifles initiative. On the other hand, if a goal is too simple then it is achieved too easily. Without a stretch there is little reward. In fact, difficult yet realistic goals produce purpose-directed lives.

We all have obstacles along the way. We must be open-minded about how we are going to accomplish our goals, and at some point we may have to change our method. We may need to back up, go around, go over or go under an obstacle rather than bull-headedly push through it. We must be malleable. We cannot allow difficulties to discourage us. Roadblocks may cause us to alter our course a bit, but we cannot let them deter us from our destination.

I have often said that we grow stronger through adversity. We become stronger physically through a weight-lifting program. Our muscles work against heavy objects. That's adversity. We get stronger mentally through the progressive difficulty of education. We don't start with calculus; we start with arithmetic. After we learn the basics, we move on to algebra, then to geometry and so on. We work our way up to calculus. In the same way, we grow stronger spiritually through the tests of life. Losing my beloved wife, Nellie, was the hardest event in my life. For a couple of years, it slowed me down; but it didn't stop me. In the end even her loss has made me stronger.

In every way—physically, morally, emotionally and spiritually—we increase our strength when life is hard; therefore, we must not dread adversity, nor can we allow it to stop us from becoming the best we can be through the steadfast pursuit of our goals. In fact, as we become stronger we can and should expand our goals. Extending our capabilities to their limits requires us to realistically reevaluate our potential.

Without intentness we can't possibly become all we can be. However, assuming our ability warrants it, we can approach the pinnacle of our profession, position or title if we have the resolve to plow through whatever life throws at us—including a curve.

She thought, "If I can just touch his robe, I will be healed" (Matthew 9:21).

CARTY

Life had thrown her a curve and she was back on her heels. She had tried to hit the pitch but it was impossible. Sometimes she wished

INTENTNESS

they'd been throwing rocks. A stoning might have been easier. At least the pain would have stopped.

During biblical times, Levitical law made life tough for a woman, especially one who was menstruating. During her period she was considered to be ceremonially unclean. Anyone who touched her would be unclean, and anything she touched was also considered unclean. If her flow continued past the usual time, she was labeled unclean until it stopped.[1]

This woman's discharge had continued for 12 terrible years. If she had been married when it started, her husband would have divorced her by now. She had no friends, nor had she felt a human touch in all those years.

She had visited all the doctors and had tried all the quacks. She had sold everything she owned, and all of her money had been spent in search of a cure. Being a woman of great resolve, when she heard Jesus was coming, she did not hesitate.

He was in the street being thronged. It was a mob scene. Everyone was trying to touch him. She was weak and anemic. There was no way she could force her way through the crowd. But she was intent, so she got down on all fours and crawled. The woman thought, *If I can just touch His robe, I will be healed.*[2]

I think she went for His ankle but got bumped and came up short. She didn't even get a chance to grab His garment. But she did touch the fringe on the bottom, and it was enough. She was healed. She knew it as she got to her feet.

"Who touched me?" Jesus asked.[3]

The woman surely thought He was angry because an unclean woman had touched Him. Peter told Jesus the whole crowd was pressing against Him.

"No, someone deliberately touched me, for I felt healing power go out from Me," Jesus responded.[4]

As Jesus turned, the crowd backed away a bit and His eyes met hers.

When the woman realized that Jesus knew, she began to tremble and fell to her knees before him. The whole crowd heard her explain why she had touched him and that she had been immediately healed.

"Daughter," he said to her, "your faith has made you well. Go in peace" (Luke 8:47-48).

The woman had the kind of faith that made her touch different from the touch of others. Power went out of Jesus to only one person in the mob. Why? She had determination, persistence, tenacity and resolve all rolled up into one word that applied to her faith. She was intent.

YOUR TURN

■ **Today's reading:** Leviticus 15:19-33; Luke 8:43-48; 11:5-13; Matthew 9:20-23

1. How do you deal with people and events that hinder you from accomplishing your main purpose? Do you need to change the way you react to distractions?

2. Describe a time when you successfully pushed through distractions and difficulties to reach your goal.

❏ I commit myself to be focused on the main objective of reaching excellence and to avoid anything less important that would keep me from reaching my greatest potential.

*Almighty Healer and Author of Faith, give me the faith
that heals my infirmities; but more than that, give me the
faith that heals my soul. Then give me intentness about the
things that are important to You. Not my will, but Your will
be done, in Jesus' name I pray. Amen.*

CONDITION

CONDITION

Mental-Moral-Physical. Rest, exercise and diet must be considered.
Moderation must be practiced. Dissipation must be eliminated.

WOODEN

We have reached the third tier and arrived at the heart of the Pyramid. This level does not only apply to athletics. The building blocks of condition, skill and team spirit apply to both individuals and teams of every kind.

By condition, I mean physical, mental, moral and spiritual fitness. Specific activities require specific conditioning. Kicking a goal, putting on a green, diving into the ocean, climbing a mountain, operating on a heart-attack victim and cross-examining a witness in a court of law—each of these examples requires different conditioning if the participant is going to be the best that he or she can be. Moreover, mental conditioning is essential. Consider the mental fortitude required to kick or putt with a championship on the line, to dive to great depths or to climb to great heights, to save a sick person's life or to deliver a closing argument.

Success also takes moral and spiritual conditioning. Rest, exercise, diet and drills can only get us so far. Moderation must be practiced. Dissipation must be eliminated. A wholesome lifestyle will produce a more successful participant. I believe there are individuals with ability that become all-Americans, all-stars and all-pros who do not take care of their bodies. They may even win championships, but they are not successes. Think of what they could be if they took care of themselves. There is a vast difference between better and best. You may be better than the rest, but you are not a success until you have made the effort to become the best you can be.

I told my players, "We want to be in the best possible condition." In my early years, I said, "Let's be in better condition than anybody else." But I changed. If the other team had more capacity for conditioning, they might have been better than we were, and there was nothing we could have done about that. So I started saying, "Let's become the best conditioned team we can possibly be. We hope that'll be better than the others, but we don't know if it will be. But let's make the effort to be in the best possible condition with the hope that we'll be better."

I also talked to my players about double responsibility—mine and theirs. As coach, my responsibility was the practices. I decided what drills to use, how long to use them, in what part of the practice to place them, how things are arranged and how long we would run.

Their responsibility was between practices. I said, "You can tear down more between practices than we can build up during practices. A lack of proper conduct, deficient rest and an improper diet will keep you from attaining and maintaining desirable conditioning. You can improve your condition, maybe, and lack some of these, but you can't attain the desirable without the physical conditioning being preceded by mental and moral conditioning."

In athletics, physical conditioning is important. That's why almost all of my basketball drills, except for free-throw shooting, were conditioning drills. But a failure to address mental, moral and spiritual conditioning will limit even the best physical conditioning.

> Physical exercise has some value, but spiritual exercise is much more important, for it promises a reward in both this life and the next (1 Timothy 4:8).

CARTY

Over the years, God has used me as His tool to save a couple of lives and quite a few souls. I'm glad I was in good condition when God called.

The greatest test of my physical conditioning came when I was in college. A teen-aged boy was in trouble in a lake about 125 yards

CONDITION

out. I got to him as he sank. I had to use a cross-chest carry to ferry him in because he fought me all the way. I have never had a more demanding physical test. If I hadn't been in great shape, the boy would have drowned.

The toughest test of my mental conditioning came when I was in my mid-30s. A woman went into shock and stopped breathing. It took eight breaths for me to bring her back. She too would have died if I hadn't been mentally ready to face a crisis situation.

My spiritual conditioning is tested all of the time. I've been in the ministry for 30 years, and there is constant temptation to sin. If I didn't maintain my spiritual fitness, I would have been out of the ministry long ago.

When God called the prophet Elijah, he too was ready.[1] Elijah was in fine physical condition. Being bald and hairy didn't slow him down.[2]

When Ahab became King, he ordered the construction of altars to false gods. God told Elijah to tell Ahab that as a result of this error, there would be several years of drought. God also told the prophet to run and hide after he had warned the king.

After confronting Ahab, Elijah fled and hung out in the wilderness. He spent some time with a single mom and her son and raised the child from the dead. When God gave Elijah another message or two for Ahab, the prophet returned to the king. It would have taken some strong spiritual conditioning to bring a child back from the dead and probably even stronger mental conditioning to face Ahab. Except for God's restraining hand, Ahab probably would have killed Elijah. Conditioning produces confidence, and Elijah was confident.

The apostle Paul had a lot in common with Elijah. Paul said, "I exercise myself, to have always a conscience void of offense toward God, and toward men."[3] The word "exercise" means to actively train, practice and struggle to give one's best, even to the point of pain. Timothy agreed with Paul when Paul said, "Physical exercise has some value, but spiritual exercise is much more important, for it promises a reward in both this life and the next."[4]

For the athlete, physical conditioning is important; but Coach got it right when he said that we won't be a success without mental, moral and spiritual conditioning as well.

It's important to be in top condition in all of these areas. When God calls, we need to be ready to respond.

YOUR TURN

■ **Today's reading:** 1 Kings 16:29—18:46; Acts 24:16; 1 Timothy 4:8

1. What do you do regularly to condition yourself physically, mentally, morally and spiritually?

2. Recall one time when your conditioning in each of the four areas paid off.

❏ I commit myself to becoming and staying fit physically, mentally, morally and spiritually.

Father in Heaven, I desire to get into the best possible physical, mental, moral and spiritual condition. Help me to use my time wisely and give me the desire to follow through until I reach my goals. I want to be ready when You call. Thank You.

SKILL

A knowledge of and the ability to properly and quickly execute the fundamentals. Be prepared and cover every little detail.

WOODEN

Skill is knowing what to do and being able to execute all of the fundamentals important to a particular task. However, skill is more than knowledge and execution. A skillful person usually has a sense of timing and the ability to quickly perform the skill.

An artist may not require timing and quickness in his or her craft, but a surgeon who performs delicate heart or brain surgery often has to make split-second decisions and perform quickly under intense pressure, or the surgeon risks losing his or her patient.

I often use driving on the Southern California freeways as an illustration of this principle. We may know how to drive, but if we don't respond quickly to tricky situations, we could be in big trouble. I pass through the intersection of the 101 and 405 freeways when traveling from where I live to UCLA. It is the busiest intersection in the nation, but only child's play compared to NASCAR tracks where drivers have to make instant decisions while traveling at almost two hundred miles an hour. There are countless activities in which we not only need to know the fundamentals, but we also must be able to execute our skill properly, quickly and at the right time.

As a coach, I sometimes had to choose between a player with skill and one with physical ability. I always chose the player with skill *and* quickness. Some great shooters do not help the team because they aren't quick enough to put up a shot when under pressure. I have had tremendously quick players who didn't help us much because they couldn't shoot. But a quick player with some basketball skills will make a bigger contribution than one who has immense skill but isn't quick. The same thinking went into my choice when it came to picking between players with size and players with quickness. Of course, I wanted as much size as possible, but quickness was more important.

Any measure of competency requires a command of the fundamentals of a given endeavor. The greater the competency the more detailed a person must be in carrying out the fundamentals. It follows that a person with limited competency can become at least somewhat skillful if he or she works on the details of the fundamentals.

Obviously we can't do much about our height or our I.Q.; however, we can affect our brainpower and our physical potential through education, training and practice. God only made one Lewis Alcindor (a.k.a. Kareem Abdul-Jabbar), one Billy Graham and one Mel Gibson. The rest of us didn't receive as much potential as the highest achievers, but each of us can still become successful. We might not become as significant as we aspire to be, but we can become the best we are capable of becoming.

Proficiency in executing the fundamentals of our craft and learning to do them quickly will go a long way toward making us a success. But to achieve significance, it's a good idea to select an activity for which God has given us at least a measure of skill.

Do you see any truly competent workers? They will serve kings rather than ordinary people (Proverbs 22:29).

CARTY

Becoming skillful takes time and hard work. Knowing where to invest that time and work becomes vital. Who wants to work diligently for countless hours and end up being mediocre, not achieving significance or not making much of a contribution with his or her life?

Not discovering our God-given talent-mix early in life is both aggravating and disappointing. Each of us senses that we are here for a purpose, and we realize that God has plans for us. Therefore, every day wasted delays the fulfillment that comes from doing what

SKILL

we have been naturally wired to do.[1]

Our potential for excellence lies in our undeveloped areas of skill—what I call our God-given hard wiring, or knack. The primary word for wisdom in the Bible best translates to "know your knack."[2] God gives the potential to be skillful. It is our job to discover our potential (the beginning of wisdom) and develop our talent to our A+ level of competency (wisdom and success). People who are biblically wise know their God-given wiring and go forward in developing their skills.

I believe the Bible teaches that each of us has been given the potential to make a significant contribution to God's Kingdom. This contribution comes about when we apply our skills and gifts. The potential to be skillful is given at physical birth, and spiritual gifts are given at the time of spiritual birth. Both skills and gifts must be discovered and then developed.

Most people want to be something other than what God has built into them. We usually aspire to accomplish something that is important in the eyes of the world. Athletes, movie stars, entertainers, writers, doctors, lawyers, important corporate presidents, heads of state and dynamic leaders tend to top the list. Our parents encourage us to climb the ladder of success. Madison Avenue tells us what's cool. Rarely do we ask God's opinion. No wonder we have trouble finding our niche.

Who thinks that God wants them to be a custodian, secretary or some other position of service? Those positions usually aren't very high on anyone's list; yet the Bible clearly states that those who serve others will be rewarded in heaven. In fact, the best leaders display a servant's attitude.[3] God favors the humble.[4] He is partial to teachers.[5] And those of the lowest rank on Earth will stand in the highest places in heaven.[6] It seems that we can set our sights as high as we want, but whatever skills we have and whatever endeavor we end up pursuing, it's best to live with the attitude of a servant.[7]

YOUR TURN

■ **Today's reading:** Exodus 28:3; 31:3; 35:10,25,35; 36:1; 1 Kings 7:14; 1 Chronicles 22:15; 28:21; 2 Chronicles 2:7, 26:15; Proverbs 22:29; 1 Corinthians 3:10; Ephesians 5:16

1. Apart from sleeping, list the top five activities in which you spend most of your time.

2. After each letter below, circle the one phrase that best describes you.

    A. People drain me, people energize me or I prefer small groups.
    B. I communicate best with: spoken words, written words or artistic expression.
    C. I like working with: things or ideas.
    D. I am most skilled: working with my hands, solving problems, selling or teaching.

3. Measure the time spent in your top five time-consuming activities against the choices above. Are you spending most of your time doing what seems to come naturally?

❑ I commit myself to developing and using the talents and gifts God has given me.

Dear Giver of Skills and Gifts, show me the area of service for which You have designed me to best fit and direct me to the place where You want me to serve. I want to develop my skills for You. Most of all, regardless of my place in the world's hierarchy, give me the attitude of a servant. Thank You.

TEAM SPIRIT SPIRIT

TEAM SPIRIT

A genuine consideration for others. An eagerness to sacrifice personal interests of glory for the welfare of all.

WOODEN

I once heard team spirit defined as a willingness to lose oneself in the group for the good of the group. I used that definition for a long time, but always thought it fell short. It took a while but I finally figured it out. I changed "willingness" to "eagerness." Willingness is more like "I will if I have to." Eagerness communicates an attitude of "I'll be happy to sacrifice personal accomplishments for the good of the team." To a degree, team spirit may overlap into enthusiasm, but I feel that this concept is significant enough to be its own block.

When we *willingly* perform a task that we should or must do for the good of the group, our heart isn't completely in it. This slight reluctance holds back our teammates. By contrast, when every member of the team *eagerly* performs every task, the group rises to a new level of accomplishment.

Team spirit is the ultimate expression of interdependence. Just as team spirit embraces an element of enthusiasm, it also houses a component of cooperation. But where cooperation makes others better, team spirit makes the group better.

My 1964 UCLA team had an unusual esprit de corps about it and was unique as an example of a group having team spirit. We didn't have a dominant player or a superstar. Any one of the starting five might have been the top scorer or the hero of the game, but none of that mattered to any of them. All they were concerned about was what they could accomplish as a team, because they knew that if the five of them operated as individuals none of them would be as effective. We didn't have a tall player to block shots if someone made a mistake on defense, so they all had to help each other. To be effective, our press also required trust and teamwork.

My 1970 UCLA team was also a good example of teamwork. Prior to 1970, we had Lewis Alcindor (Kareem Abdul-Jabbar), and he could cover for a lot of mistakes. Lewis got most of the media attention, and deservedly so. I'm not aware of his teammates being critical of it. But everybody wondered how we would do when he left, and most people thought we would fall on our face. I think the 1970 team wanted to show the world that they could get along without the big guy. And they all knew they could accomplish much more as a team than they could as individuals, so they became one of my best teams.

Team spirit is consideration, respect and dignity for others. I believe that if heads of state throughout this troubled world of ours truly had more consideration for others, our problems would not be as severe. I'm not saying we wouldn't be without problems. Trouble will always exist. But if we display true consideration for others, most of our problems will be manageable.

Patriotism is team spirit in its grandest form. Today our team spirit as a nation is being put to the test to see how much we are willing to pay for our freedom.

> If one part suffers, all the parts suffer with it, and if one part is honored, all the parts are glad. Now all of you together are Christ's body, and each one of you is a separate and necessary part of it (1 Corinthians 12:26-27).

CARTY

During the Iraqi war, coalition forces went to great lengths to minimize collateral damage. To accomplish this, each nation's military forces and each division within those forces had to cooperate with the others, functioning as a team.

Individual airplanes carried out the most sophisticated attacks, delivering single, precisely targeted bombs or missiles. However, to

TEAM SPIRIT

reach each target each attack airplane had the help of other aircraft.

Standard tactics call first on defense suppression aircraft. An EF-111 aircraft would jam the Iraqi long-range radar, forcing its crews to rely upon battery-powered radar. Next, an F4-G Wild Weasel would fire a missile to knock out that radar, effectively grounding the Iraqi missiles.

To protect the attack aircraft, fighter planes came next. Finally, the bomber would arrive. The planes came from different bases and traveled at various speeds, but they always arrived on time, thanks to the AWACS (airborne warning and control system) command planes acting as traffic cops in the crowded and unfriendly skies.[1]

No single airplane, pilot or role was more important than another. The various forces functioned as a team rather than as individuals, accomplishing much more, seeing much less collateral damage and suffering far fewer losses.

That's the way the Body of Christ (the Church) should operate. No one role is more important than another. In 1 Corinthians 3:7-8, Paul drives home the point:

> The ones who do the planting or watering aren't important, but God is important because he is the one who makes the seed grow. The one who plants and the one who waters work as a team with the same purpose.

God wants us to know that the evangelist isn't any more important than the person who disciples another, nor is the one who prepared the soil more valuable than the harvester. All are equally important members of the team. People who have heard me preach have often referred to my contribution as fertilizer. The point is, to God my contribution is no more valuable than yours, but neither is it less.

The apostle Paul emphasized this point: "Some of us are Jews, some are Gentiles, some are slaves, and some are free. But we have all been baptized into Christ's body by one Spirit, and we have all received the same Spirit" (1 Corinthians 12:13). In some households, the master was being discipled by his slave, and Gentiles were discipling Jews—for the culture of the day, absurd considerations that were outside the concept of team spirit. But God obviously approved.

Don't think more highly of yourself than you ought,[2] but don't think less of yourself either. Be an eager team member, not reluctant or just willing. God wants your heart, and God's team needs your contribution.

YOUR TURN

■ **Today's reading:** John 15:12; 1 Peter 1:22; 1 Thessalonians 3:12; 1 Corinthians 3:6-9; 12:12-27; Romans 12:3-5,10

1. List the groups to which you belong (church, parachurch, community, school, etc.). What role do you play in each group?

2. Do your current roles best utilize your spiritual gifts and natural talents? How can you be a better team member?

❑ I commit myself to finding the best avenue for maximizing my contribution as an enthusiastic member of the Body of Christ.

Almighty Creator, You made us to best function interdependently.
Give me an eagerness to contribute my talents and gifts to
Your body of believers that we might function as a team and
accomplish more for the Kingdom collectively than we could ever
accomplish individually. Thank You.

POISE

Just being yourself. Being at ease in any situation.
Never fighting yourself.

WOODEN

Two blocks form the next-to-the-highest level of the Pyramid of Success: poise and confidence. These two qualities will be the natural outgrowth of having the other blocks in their proper place. We won't have either if we don't have the others. In fact, poise is a composite, or the result, of other blocks.

Most people think of poise as calm, self-assured dignity; but I call it "just being you." When we have poise, we're not acting, faking or pretending. We're not trying to be something we're not, nor are we attempting to live up to others' expectations. Therefore, when we are being who we really are, we'll have a greater likelihood of functioning nearer our own level of competency.

If someone who lived in a rural area was invited to the Governor's Ball, that person would adjust his or her outward appearance and behavior to fit the social constructs of the event; but with poise the person doesn't even attempt to change who he or she really is. If we have poise, we won't be concerned about what others think. Outside influences won't change who we are or what we try to be. We'll never try to be anything other than who we are. The young people of today would say to a poised person, "You're not a poser." Poise keeps us true to ourselves. We're at ease with ourselves, and as long as we're at ease with ourselves, we're going to function nearer to our own ability.

Poise greatly depends upon two nearby blocks: self-control and confidence, which are primary ingredients of poise. The person with poise is quietly in control at all times because he or she is confident. In fact, a fully prepared person is more apt to be confident. The confidence that comes from thorough preparation and the discipline of

POISE

self-control usually results in poise.

I've often been asked, "Aren't these difficult characteristics to achieve?"

Yes, and they should be. They're good qualities, and good qualities should be difficult to attain. Being difficult makes achieving them all the more worthwhile. How do we acquire them?

This question deserves a complete answer: We acquire them by being industrious, by being enthusiastic, by being friendly, by being loyal, by being cooperative, by maintaining self-control, by being alert and alive and constantly observant, by having initiative and not being afraid to fail while realizing that we are imperfect and we will fail on occasion, by being intent and determined to reach realistic objectives and by being competitive in whatever we're doing, by being in the best possible condition for whatever we're doing, by being skilled and being able to execute not only properly but quickly, and by being imbued with team spirit and consideration for others.

In other words, if we do the work required on the three foundational layers of the Pyramid of Success, we'll likely have poise.

I, the Lord, am your God, who brought you from the land of Egypt so you would no longer be slaves. I have lifted the yoke of slavery from your neck so you can walk free with your heads held high (Leviticus 26:13).

CARTY

A shepherd and an orphan are among the many biblical characters with calm, assured dignity. They obtained their poise from God, not through their own efforts. When God's got you, you don't have to trust yourself or be concerned about what anyone else thinks.

Moses had herded sheep for 40 years, but he wasn't worried about what pharaoh thought. Moses even had a speech impediment, and I think that's why he balked a bit before first going to talk to the ruler.[1] Nonetheless, after confessing his weakness, Moses stood up to the monarch ten times and demanded that pharaoh let the Jewish people go. Moses wasn't intimidated and demonstrated the poise that comes when we do God's will.

Esther was another of God's people whose poise resulted in great success. She was an orphaned Jewish girl who was raised and adopted by a relative. Esther had beauty in form and face,[2] but there was much more to her. There must have been grace, charm and unbelievable poise in Esther because she always obtained favor in the sight of all who looked at her.[3]

The king was a male chauvinist simpleton and a narcissist lacking in discernment. Whoever had his ear could make him flip-flop on issues and decrees. Esther saw this firsthand. The king's prime minister wanted to kill Esther's relatives and all the Jewish people, so he coerced the king to sign a decree. It was Esther's poise, combined with courage, that God used to turn the tables on the villain, have him hanged on the gallows he had built for her relatives, and save the Jewish people from annihilation.

Esther was God's instrument to avert the destruction of the Jews. Because of what she did, the Jewish people celebrate the annual Feast of Purim in memory of their deliverance. They wouldn't be too far off if they'd called it the feast of poise. After all, that was the quality in Esther's life that God used to save them.

Moses and Esther demonstrated remarkable combinations of control and confidence—the primary components in poise. They displayed courage, too. When these components are rooted in Christ, rather than self, we have a far firmer foundation upon which to achieve success. For believers, the yoke of the slavery of sin has been lifted. That means we can always walk with our heads held high, regardless of our backgrounds.[4] In addition, along with being controlled by God and placing our confidence in Him, knowing we're forgiven will also contribute to our poise.

YOUR TURN

■ **Today's reading:** Exodus 4:10; 5:1; Joshua 2:1-21; 6:15-25; Esther

1. To answer the following questions, rate yourself on a scale of 1 to 10 by circling the number that best fits you.

   • Do you usually prepare or wing it?

   Prepare   **Wing it**
   1 - 2 - 3 - 4 - 5 - 6 - 7 - 8 - 9 - 10

   • Do you usually have your emotions under control?

   Under control   **Lack of control**
   1 - 2 - 3 - 4 - 5 - 6 - 7 - 8 - 9 - 10

   • When it comes to your relationship with God, are you poised, or are you a poser?

   Poised   **Posing**
   1 - 2 - 3 - 4 - 5 - 6 - 7 - 8 - 9 - 10

2. Based on the above self-evaluation, what do you need to work on most?

❑ I will continue to pursue excellence in the qualities that will produce poise in all aspects of my life.

Almighty Creator of ultimate courage, I place my confidence in You and my faith in Christ. I want to be controlled by Your Holy Spirit. Give me the poise that comes with leading a Spirit-controlled life. Thank You, blessed Lord.

CONFIDENCE

Respect without fear. May come from being prepared and keeping all things in proper perspective.

WOODEN

In college, students can enroll in speech classes to learn how to improve the way they present themselves. Charm schools and finishing schools can instruct people in ways to walk, look and act; but it is a mistake to think that any school can teach either poise or confidence. Poise and confidence simply can't be taught.

Remember that my definition of poise is "just being you." That means that any class that trains people to do something other than be themselves isn't teaching poise or confidence; it's teaching acting.

One of my favorite maxims is "Failing to prepare is preparation for failure." Poise and confidence come with proper preparation. When we are as prepared as we know how to be, and we know that we have the tools to handle most of the unknowns that might come our way, we can go into an event, a job, a meeting, a show or any other venue with total confidence.

I always wanted my teams to be confident, but not overconfident. I did not want them to be cocky or whistling in the dark. Solid respect without fear is what I was after. I wanted them to believe in themselves without being self-centered, intimidated or naive.

I hoped my teams would go onto the floor with style and confidence. Our assuredness needed to so take over the arena that our opponent and the crowd would wonder how we could be so well prepared and so sure of our performance, even before the game started.

A positive approach to teaching is the best way to build confidence. The way I taught rebounding was controversial, but it was positive. Most other coaches teach what is called "boxing out." In other words, when it comes to rebounding, a player must keep his opponent from getting the ball. That's not positive. I taught my players to get between their opponent and the ball, and to go get the ball. I wanted my boys to be thinking, *I'm going to get the ball.* I didn't want them lamenting, *I have to keep my man from getting the ball.* I kept very good records over the years and there were very few games in which we were outrebounded. Positive teaching produced more confidence in my players, and it made us better rebounders.

I learned something from baseball that helped me with basketball and improved my confidence as a coach. Baseball managers know which play to call to give them the best odds of success. Of course, they don't know if their decision will work, but they do know that over time they will succeed more often if they play the odds. When I applied this approach to basketball, I had more confidence. My players had confidence, too. They knew that the coaches would never do anything or make any decisions that didn't give them the best opportunity to do their best, as a team. If our best was good enough to win, we won. If it wasn't, we lost; but we always tried to do our best and let the results take care of themselves.

> For I am convinced that neither death, nor life, nor angels, nor principalities, nor things present, nor things to come, nor powers, nor height, nor depth, nor any other created thing, will be able to separate us from the love of God, which is in Christ Jesus our Lord (Romans 8:38-39, *NASB*).

CARTY

Stephen was a picture of confidence. He stood solid before the first rock hit, did not waver as a hailstorm of stones flew toward him and remained confident even when the last rock struck his body with a thud. Stephen had delivered the first defense of the Christian faith, and as a result, he was stoned. The first Christian martyr, he had done his best, lost the battle, but won the war.

Three methods of stoning were prevalent in Stephen's day: In the official method, a scaffold was built about the height of a basketball hoop. The accused was tied, escorted to the top and pushed. An accuser would try to drop a big rock on him or her. With pomp and circumstance, everybody would stand in a circle and throw rocks until the accused was dead.

A more common mode of stoning was done in a pit. Most towns had a stoning pit. It was cheaper than building a scaffold. The pit was 8 to 10 feet deep and 15 to 20 feet wide. The accused was thrown in and the townspeople threw rocks until the person was dead.

A third way was a plain old lynch-mob style of stoning. People would form a circle around the accused and chuck rocks at him or her. People didn't like this method much because if you side armed a rock and missed, somebody on the other side of the circle might be hit.

Although Stephen was one of the first of seven Early Church deacons, he became better known as a preacher. When local Pharisees attempted to debate him, they lost—big time. In retaliation, they did the same thing to Stephen that they did to Jesus. They got false witnesses to testify against him and then put him on trial. During the trial, Stephen delivered what many consider to be the best defense of the faith ever.[1] After he had delivered his speech, Stephen was stoned to death. Because Stephen's accusers wanted his death to appear legitimate, he was probably killed in a pit.

Stephen exhibited confidence. He was selected as a deacon because he was of good reputation, was filled with the Holy Spirit and displayed wisdom.[2] When he preached, he demonstrated grace and power, and through him the Holy Spirit performed great wonders and signs.[3] When accused, he remained confident in his faith.[4] When he spoke, it was obvious that he was filled with the Holy Spirit.[5] Stephen was confident that he was going to heaven; in fact, he said so just before the last rock hit him.[6]

Stephen was always prepared. He knew the Scriptures, had God's wisdom at his fingertips and stayed filled with the Holy Spirit. No wonder he exhibited confidence in each setting in which he found himself, including the last one at the bottom of the stoning pit.

Do you have Stephen's kind of confidence? If not, put your faith in Jesus Christ and you will be given the confidence that, through the power of the Holy Spirit, absolutely nothing, including death, will ever separate you from the love of God.

YOUR TURN

■ **Today's reading:** Romans 5:1-5; 8:31-39; 1 John 5:13-15; 1 Corinthians 2:1-5; Acts 6:1-8:3; 22:19-20

1. On a scale of 1 to 10, how convinced are you that nothing will be able to separate you from the love of God, which is in Christ Jesus your Lord? _____

2. On a scale of 1 to 10, when presented with an opportunity to share your faith, how often do you come through? _____

3. On a scale of 1 to 10, how convinced are you that your sin is really forgiven? _____

4. On a scale of 1 to 10, if you had to reject Jesus or die, what number best indicates what you would probably do? _____

❏ I commit myself to regularly reading God's Word and to living in the confidence of God's forgiveness by regularly confessing my sins.

Great Giver of confidence and assurance, prepare me with Your Holy Word, fill me with Your Holy Spirit and give me wisdom to confidently turn to You like Stephen did. I know that You will never let me be separated from Your love. Thank You.

COMPETITIVE GREATNESS

Be at your best when your best is needed. Enjoyment of a difficult challenge.

WOODEN

If we demonstrate all of the preceding qualities, we have the potential for success; but without competitive greatness, we won't be the best we can be. Competitive greatness is the pinnacle of the Pyramid. With competitive greatness, we can deliver our best when our best is needed; at the same time, we can make those around us better, too. A person with this quality loves a challenge—the tougher the better.

Many superstars possess competitive greatness.[1] Michael Jordan, Larry Bird and Magic Johnson instantly come to mind. It seems that God endowed each of them with a quality that is almost unexplainable. They seemed to enjoy the difficult situations. The tougher the circumstances, the higher they rose; and in doing so, they always made those around them better.

In the sixth game of the 1998 NBA finals, Michael Jordan had the flu, yet he played. During time-outs, toward the end of the game, he would almost pass out, yet he continued. When he finally won the game—scoring his forty-fifth point of the game with 5.2 seconds to go—he could no longer stand; his teammates had to hug him while he was seated. He was completely spent—he had left it all on the floor—but he had willed his team to play their best. That is competitive greatness.

Bill Russell wasn't as gifted as some other superstars, but through his competitive spirit he willed his team to 13 championships. His contemporary Wilt Chamberlain was more gifted physically, but Wilt didn't have that extra quality that Russell had.

Having competitive greatness does not always mean that you are the one who scores the most points or hits the winning shot. Lewis

90

Alcindor (Kareem Abdul-Jabbar) could have set every college scoring record in the book. However, he didn't. He could see the big picture, always reigning in his own play for the sake of elevating the play of his teammates. As a result, he was rewarded with a championship every year he played. Only UCLA basketball players can claim that they won it all every year they played.

When I played basketball at Purdue, I was considered to be a somewhat intense competitor; but if you had talked to people about me as a coach prior to 1963, they wouldn't have given me such accolades. Those who knew me well knew my competitive nature, but the general public equates championships with success. While we won a lot of games in the early years, UCLA's first basketball championship did not come until 1964.

I was at peace with myself before we ever won a national championship. I didn't feel more at peace with myself or feel more successful after we started winning more championships. People who I appreciate the most are those who said, "Johnny never changed. He was the same after he won his trophies as he was before." I like that. I hope it's true.

We don't have to be superstars or win championships to reach competitive greatness. All we have to do is learn to rise to every occasion, give our best effort and make those around us better as we do it. It's not about winning. It's about learning to give all we have to give.

"Don't worry about a thing," David told Saul. "I'll go fight this Philistine!" (1 Samuel 17:32).

CARTY

For Norm Evans, this highest building block took shape when he played college football at Texas Christian University under a coach who had much the same outlook as John Wooden has.

One day after practice, Norm and his coach walked off the field together. The coach put his arm around Norm, looked his player in the eye and tenderly said, "Laddie, you didn't give me your best today." The coach patted Norm and walked off.

Norm cried and then changed his approach to practice. From that day forward, whether in practice or in a game, he gave it his all. For 14 seasons, Norm was an undersized lineman in the NFL. To survive at that level for so long took competitive greatness. In 1972, he was a vital cog on the offensive line of the undefeated Miami Dolphins. His competitive spirit had rubbed off on his teammates.

Like Norm, David was undersized. And like Norm, David came to a day that would determine whether he had competitive greatness. The story is told in 1 Samuel 16:1–17:58.

When David was a youth, his brothers thought he was a punk. Nonetheless, he had been selected by God and anointed by Samuel to be the next king. While he waited to be crowned, he had a part-time gig playing lead guitar for Saul. David had experienced God's protection and had learned something about his competitive spirit when he killed a lion and a bear in order to defend his sheep during his gig as a shepherd. A turning point came when he was delivering food to his older brothers who were on the front line of a battle.

At nine feet in height, the Philistine champion, Goliath, towered over everyone. His armor alone weighed 125 pounds. This was one big dude. He had taunted the Israelites and blasphemed God. Saul and his army were terrified and deeply shaken. When David heard about Goliath's behavior, he was ticked; his competitive juices started flowing.

Before facing Goliath, David turned down Saul's offer to wear armor—it would slow him down, he reasoned. He'd been taught to be quick, but not hurry. For weapons, David took a sling and a stone. He rocked Goliath's world, hitting him right between the eyes.

David had demonstrated poise when he rejected Saul's armor. In battle, he wanted to be himself. David demonstrated confidence knowing that God had delivered him in the past and—since God had anointed him to be king—that He would protect him from harm. It took competitive greatness to stand up for God at a time when no one else would. Moreover, David made his teammates better. After he killed Goliath, the offensive line of the Israelite army defeated the Philistines.

We are in a battle, and the enemy is trash-talking God.[2] If that doesn't tick you off, it should. If you are a Christian, the Holy Spirit has anointed you with power. You can take on giants. Think about what God has done for you in the past. It will give you confidence that He will also act in the future.

YOUR TURN

■ **Today's reading:** 1 Samuel 16:1—17:58; 1 Corinthians 9:24-27; Ephesians 6:10-17

1. List a few times when you have rallied those around you. List a few times when you have boldly stood up for God.

2. Were these events in the distant past or are they more current? Is your boldness increasing or decreasing? If you need more boldness, how are you going to go about attaining it?

❏ I commit myself to giving my all for God.

> *Almighty Father in heaven, give me a competitive spirit*
> *so that I might successfully defend the faith and unite believers*
> *in the battle for souls. Whenever I falter, remind me of*
> *what You have done for me in the past so that my courage*
> *is built up for the future. Thank You.*

COMPETITIVE GREATNESS

AMBITION

(for noble goals)

WOODEN

To hold a structure of bricks (or blocks) together, the mason applies mortar around each layer. In the Pyramid of Success, character qualities bond the 15 building blocks, thus symbolizing mortar. These character qualities actually run throughout the Pyramid and help us advance toward the apex.

Except for faith and patience (which I place at the top of the Pyramid), the other bonding agents can be moved and still support the Pyramid. Actually, I have shifted the order through the years, but I've come to prefer the arrangement I use in this book. Let's start with "ambition."

Ambition is a feeling or a desire to achieve a goal. Usually that goal revolves around a person's definition of success or greatness. I believe we are most likely to succeed when ambition is focused on noble and worthy purposes and outcomes rather than on goals set out of selfishness. If our ambition is to be highly publicized, receive a lot of recognition, attain a position of power or prestige, or make a lot of money, we do not have noble goals. If we are focused away from ourselves and on the team and others, we possess noble goals.

When we have noble goals, we prioritize the bigger picture. As a result, people with noble goals tend to bring the team or others along with them while they climb the Pyramid of Success.

Ambition can be either a good thing or a bad thing. It depends on what we're ambitious about. We should never let ambition cause us to sacrifice our integrity or diminish our efforts in other aspects of the Pyramid. However, we need to remember that we never reach a serious goal unless we have the intention of doing so. The seriousness of that intention is what I call ambition.

Make no mistake about it: I wanted to win a national championship. I set goals that I thought might eventually put us in position to win one, and it turned out pretty well. However, I would have been at ease if we hadn't won a championship, because my significance and self-worth were never attached to winning. I just wanted me, as an individual, and my players, as a team, to improve.

Our championships came as the by-product of meeting lesser goals of measurable, year-over-year improvement. I wanted to get the best possible players and help them become the best they could become as players and as citizens. I also wanted them to improve as a team. If we could do that, whatever followed would be icing on the cake as far as I was concerned. Championships were never the cake; they were the icing. Doing our best was the cake.

With talent, we might get to the top and be esteemed in the world's eyes; but it takes character to stay there. It's true; if we operate with the selfish personal ambition that is all about us, we might get to the top of the heap, but we will never reach the pinnacle of the Pyramid.

> For wherever there is jealousy and selfish ambition, there
> you will find disorder and every kind of evil (James 3:16).

CARTY

Once upon a time there was a guy who made it to the top of the heap, but lost by a hair. It's a tragic story of selfish ambition run amuck.[1]

Absalom was David's third son. We start to see who Absalom really was after his sister was raped by his half brother. Absalom had him killed.

Afterward, Absalom ran and hid for three years until his father cooled off. David missed his son and allowed him to return to Jerusalem, but gave him the cold shoulder for two more years. That

AMBITION

was not a good thing to do to an intelligent, scheming, vengeful man who had no fear and no sense of right and wrong. Absalom decided to get even, but in so doing he allowed his selfish ambition to get the best of him. The young man decided that he wanted to be king.

Absalom was a promoter. To impress the crowds, he rode a chariot with 50 outriders. And he was slick. With his natural good looks and flowing long hair, people trusted this clever, silver-tongued weasel. Taking advantage of his natural assets, he started a subversive program of subtle insinuation that would make a presidential election look tame. Absalom's plan was so effective that he pulled off a bloodless coup, overthrew his dad, David, and had himself crowned king in Hebron, the city where his father had also been crowned.[2]

King David had defeated bigger armies, but he didn't want to hurt his own people—he especially didn't want to harm his overindulged son, whom he still loved way too much. Moreover, David did not want the battle to occur in Jerusalem, the city he loved. As a result, David put off a confrontation as long as he could. Finally, after some wonderful espionage and delightful intrigue that would make novelist Tom Clancy proud, it was time to do battle. Twenty thousand people died, including Absalom.

David appointed three generals for the battle, including Joab. It seems that while retreating, Absalom's hair got wrapped in a tree but his mount kept going. Joab found the would-be king dangling from the tree and shish-kebabed him three times. Thus, Absalom suffered the consequences of his selfish ambition. As it is written in James, jealousy and selfish ambition lead to disorder and evil of all kinds.[3]

The Bible has the answer to the problem.

Don't copy the behavior and customs of this world, but let God transform you into a new person by changing the way you think. Then you will know what God wants you to do, and you will know how good and pleasing and perfect his will really is (Romans 12:2).

YOUR TURN

- **Today's reading:** James 3:13—4:10; Romans 12:1-2; 2 Samuel 13:1—18:18

1. List the current driving forces in your life. How much of your ambition in these areas is self-centered and how much is noble?

2. Do you need to rethink and redirect your goals? In what area of your life will you begin this process? What will your first steps to change be?

❏ I commit myself to putting aside selfish goals and to setting new, noble goals that will help other people and bring glory to God.

Almighty God and Heavenly Father, show me if selfish ambition is getting in the way of our relationship and help me to set noble goals that will be pleasing in Your sight and bring glory to You. Thank You.

AMBITION

SINCERITY

(keeps friends)

WOODEN

Friendship, loyalty, cooperation and team spirit each occupy building blocks in the Pyramid of Success. What do these blocks say about success? They tell us that we cannot become successful unless we interact with others. Sincerity is the mortar that binds together the blocks of friendship, loyalty, cooperation and team spirit. Therefore, sincerity is also necessary to reach the apex.

Sincerity may not make a friend, but it will keep one. It often takes a while to be validated, but once a person knows that our word, character and steadfastness have withstood the tests of life, a firm friendship can be established and maintained.

When we realize that a friend can be counted on during times of need, when we see that his or her values don't blow around in the breeze, and when he or she stands up for us, we are far more apt to stand up for him or her—and vice versa.

In the military, the soldiers following a sincere leader will do more for him or her than they will for an insincere one, especially when under fire. Sincerity works the same way on the basketball court. Players will do more for a coach who sincerely cares about them than they will for one who is using his or her players as a stepping-stone to get a better job or accumulate a better record. When players know the coach cares about them as individuals, they will get closer to giving their personal bests. Sincerity is the agent that brings this dynamic to life.

Achievement and recognition will alienate some people through no fault of our own. There are always some people who want to bring us down and keep us down, and there are others who want to keep us from going up. Those are not friendships based on sincerity.

Like anyone else, I have people in my life who don't like me or who disagree with certain things I do. When I have become aware of a problem or major disagreement, I have attempted to reconcile with the person who has been hurt or who is at odds with me. I have reached out in all sincerity; yet, in some cases, it has been to no avail. I wish it were otherwise, but we cannot force anyone to mend differences.

Having people in our lives who continue to be alienated from us doesn't mean that we can't be successful. However, there is a caution: If we find that it is the norm for us to leave people floating, drifting and drowning like debris in our wake, then we aren't a success, regardless of the recognition the world gives us. Without sincerity, we will alienate people needlessly. With sincerity, we will have an abundance of friends and be one step closer to success.

> The purpose of my instruction is that all the Christians there would be filled with love that comes from a pure heart, a clear conscience, and sincere faith (1 Timothy 1:5).

CARTY

If I am talking with a friend who is an older person, like me, I'll often use the words, "Stay faithful and finish well." It is what I sincerely want to do, so I encourage them to do the same.

Most of the time, I just close my letters with "Sincerely." For me, this expression means that what I just wrote is true. The word "sincerely" means "without wax." Its origins come from the Latin words *sine cera*.

Roman artists would often fill a chipped statue with wax and pass it off as being good. Potters would frequently take vessels that had hairline cracks from improper firing and fill the gaps with wax. In time, the wax would melt and the vessel would leak. Potential buyers would hold pottery to the light to look for cracks filled with wax.

Commercially, the practice of filling in mistakes with wax

SINCERITY

became so commonplace that a tested vessel (a container held up to the light) was called "sincere," or without wax. Biblically, the concept translates as "without blemish, pure, wholesome, genuine, true or sincere." John the Baptist was the embodiment of all of these words.

John was sincere when he said of Jesus, "He must become greater and greater, and I must become less and less" (John 3:30). He understood his role and he accepted it willingly. Humility is a waxless trait.

John was sincere when he called Herod on the carpet because Herod had married his own brother's wife.[1] John wouldn't sugarcoat sin, so he put his life on the line and called it like he saw it. As a result of John's stand, Herod's wife, Herodias, had him killed.[2] John the Baptist preferred to be waxless and headless rather than alive, cracked and full of wax.

At the end of John's short life, Jesus called him the greatest man ever born of a woman.[3] The Son of God held John the Baptist to the light and found him to be almost without wax. Of course, like all of us, John started off cracked. He had a sin nature that he could trace back to Adam. Jesus' accolades would seem to indicate that John the Baptist, who was also known as the forerunner of Christ, came closer than anyone to being waxless.

Would you like to take greater control over your sin nature? Would you like to decrease the need for wax to fill the cracks in your life? When exposed to the light of the Son, Jesus, how often is your faith found to be sincere?

After you confess your sin, you are clean and pure.[4] Your goal ought to be to sin less and confess faster after you mess up. Increasing control over sin and rushing back to God quicker when you do sin are two good measurements of a sincere faith.

YOUR TURN

■ **Today's reading:** Matthew 11:7-11; 14:1-12; John 3:22-30; Mark 6:14-29; Hebrews 10:22

1. Relate one incident in which you stood for what was right or truthful, but there was a cost that you had to pay.

2. When you sin, how fast do you go to God and ask for forgiveness? What can you do to reduce the number of cracks in your life and become more waxless?

❑ I commit myself to becoming a sincere person in every area of my life, even when there is a cost.

Dear Father of Faith, I want my faith to be sincere. Forgive me of my sins and help me gain a greater measure of control over my fallen nature through the power of Your Holy Spirit. And Lord, give me a passion to stay in Your will for increasing periods of time. Thank You.

SINCERITY

ADAPTABILITY

(to any situation)

WOODEN

Adaptability is being able to adjust to any situation at any given time.

In life, we all know that we can only be sure of a few things, specifically death and taxes. We can also count on change. We need to recognize change, grow with it and learn from it. Since change is inevitable, people who are inflexible, bull-headed or stubborn will never make it to the apex of the Pyramid. If we want to succeed, we must readily adapt to circumstances as they unfold—this includes both what we cannot change and what will take some time to change.

Life itself underscores this dynamic. Think of the seasons through which each of us passes. When our parents take us out of our crib and stand us upright, we must adapt by trying to take our first steps, or we fall down. As teens, we must adjust to one bodily change after another. As adults, we go to college, get a job, get married, have children, send our children off to college, have grandchildren, retire and so forth. Each season brings about change, much of which we cannot control. If we fail to adapt, we fail to move forward.

Being malleable is a must, not only as we move from one season of life to another, but also every day. When I moved from Indiana to UCLA, I had to adapt. People in Indiana loved basketball. In California, there was not as much interest. In Indiana, I had the finest facilities and six baskets to use in practice. In California, I had to adapt. We had an old gym and only two baskets. Moreover, we had to share the floor with the gymnastics and wrestling teams. In the early years at UCLA, we did not have a home court for games. I had to adapt. I even had to sweep the floor.

Every season, I had to adapt to the personnel who were under my supervision. When Lewis Alcindor came to UCLA, I had to adjust my offense to take advantage of his strengths. I even adjusted my coaching style, bringing Jay Carty into the gym to practice one-on-one with Lew.

To take advantage of changing circumstances, we must survey the situation and then make the necessary adjustments. We may need to bring in new personnel; we may need to change a routine, or we may need to change our actions.

We can plan a road trip down to the last detail, but the unexpected will always arise. When the unexpected happens, we must adapt. If the airplane arrives late or it is snowing, we must adapt our schedule. If when we arrive at our hotel, other guests are making noise, we must adapt our routine. If the only restaurant open serves burgers and fries, we must adapt our diet. If we do not adapt, we will get left behind.

We change what we can, but if we get too concerned, involved and engrossed in circumstances over which we have no control or can't change, those circumstances are going to have a negative impact on events and outcomes we can control.

To the weak I became weak, that I might win the weak; I have become all things to all men, that I may by all means save some (1 Corinthians 9:22, *NASB*).

CARTY

In biblical days, most outsiders were jealous and hated the Jewish people, whom God had chosen as His prize. The Jewish people were equally bigoted. As they saw it, there were two groups: them and everybody else. Anyone who was not a Jew was a Gentile. The social divide was so large that Jewish people wouldn't enter a Gentile's house, nor would they fraternize with them. In fact, it was forbidden for a Jewish person to eat a meal with a Gentile.

Jesus broke this unspoken rule many times, most notably when he had dinner with sinners. His huge social no-no caused a stir, especially among legalistic Jews called the Pharisees; however, few if any of His own followers took the cue and permanently adjusted their behavior toward Gentiles—at least not right away. Peter figured it out first, and he shook some trees. Then Paul blew open the barn doors.

God spoke to Peter and taught him a lesson: "If God says something is acceptable, don't say that it isn't" (Acts 10:15). God immediately tested Peter, sending some Gentiles to his door. To appreciate God's choice of Peter, we need to know that loudmouthed Pete had a habit of sticking his foot in his mouth. This time he got it right. He went against his upbringing, against his training and totally against his prejudice. He obeyed God and he adapted. It's not easy to overcome the training and traditions of a lifetime, but he changed because God said it was time to change.

Peter visited Cornelius, a Gentile, and he declared:

> You know it is against the Jewish laws for me to come into a Gentile home like this. But God has shown me that I should never think of anyone as impure. . . . I see very clearly that God doesn't show partiality. In every nation he accepts those who fear him and do what is right (Acts 10:28,34-35).

Paul one-upped Peter. The apostle not only adapted to this new way of seeing Gentiles, but he also added thunder: "There is no longer Jew or Gentile, slave or free, male or female. For you are all Christians—you are one in Christ Jesus" (Galatians 3:28).

Adapting may be as simple as adjusting to an opponent's fullcourt press in a basketball game, or it may mean changing an ingrained belief or old habit because God says He wants to move forward. Whether the issue is small or large, humdrum or close to our heart, the ability to adapt is a vital cohesive in holding together the blocks of the Pyramid.

YOUR TURN

■ **Today's reading:** Acts 10:1-48; 15:6-11; Galatians 2:1-10; 3:23–4:7; 1 Corinthians 9:20-22

1. What criteria do you use to determine when you need to adapt? List a few significant times in which you adapted, even if you did so reluctantly.

2. How do you respond when God asks you to adjust a habit, attitude or behavioral pattern in your life?

❏ I commit myself to being an instrument of change for truth and righteousness, even in circumstances requiring me to change my thinking.

Dear Creator of all People, open my eyes to the changes
I need to make in my life. I want to adapt to be all things to
all people so that I might be able to effectively share Your truth
with those You place in my path. Thank You.

ADAPTABILITY

HONESTY

(in thought and action)

WOODEN

Honesty is doing the things that we know are right and not giving into the temptation to do the things that we know are wrong. Honesty must occur at all times, in both thought and action. Honest people stay on the narrow way, regardless of the consequences. If we are honest, our integrity will not allow us to compromise—ever. Honest people don't lie to others, to themselves or to God.

A dishonest act is an attempt to deceive someone. It is possible to be so deceptive that we even deceive ourselves. We do this when we attempt to justify a lie because of circumstances or as payback when someone has been dishonest with us. Dishonesty—no matter the reason—destroys our credibility, ruins our reputation and costs us our self-respect.

The clearest form of dishonesty is an outright lie. But that is not the only form. Consider this: When I was a high school coach, four of my five starters came down with measles and had to miss a game. The opposing coach ran up the score that night. I was not happy and got revenge. In striking back, I wasn't true to my values, and I later apologized for my actions.

At UCLA, I was tempted to be dishonest many times. Mostly, I resisted, but there was one situation of which I am not very proud. An opposing coach repeatedly sent the wrong shooter to the free-throw line. (In basketball, the player who is fouled is supposed to shoot free throws, but this coach would slip in a player with a better shooting percentage than the one who was fouled.) Since the opposing coach got away with this illegal maneuver, I tried it, too. But I was not so good at being stealthy—and I got caught. I regret giving in to temptation, not only because I got caught, but primarily because I did not stay true to my standards.

In another situation, I violated college basketball rules and bailed one of my players out of jail. I recount the full story in *Coach Wooden One-On-One*. The important point here is that I broke the rules to do what I thought was best for the player; but I never hid what I had done, and I was prepared to face any sanction that might have come down on UCLA and me. Yes, I broke the rules, but I was honest about my reasons and my actions.

Being tempted to be dishonest is not the problem. We all face that. The lesson to learn is how to resist the temptation when it comes. I can't recall ever being tempted to steal money, but I have been tempted to discredit someone. A particular person was attempting to harm my reputation and I wanted to get back at him. I didn't actually do it—*but I wanted to.*

Honesty is not only the best policy, but it is also the best therapy. Telling the truth and being true to ourselves not only enhances our relations with others and with God, but it also makes us feel good about ourselves.

Remember, it is sin to know what you ought to do and then not do it (James 4:17).

CARTY

We can all identify with Coach. At one time or another each of us has been tempted to mislead, lie or cheat. We usually don't have a lot to say about when the temptation will come—thoughts just pop into our mind. We can even hoodwink ourselves with sneaky justifications, such as *No one will notice* or *A little white lie will not hurt anyone* or *Everyone does it!*

Simply having a thought is not the problem; giving it room to grow is. We can control whether we dwell upon a particular temptation or vanquish it. The longer we hold on to a thought, the more likely we are to act upon it. Staying honest is as simple as discerning between good and bad thoughts, and not allowing the bad ones to linger.

Much of being honest has to do with self-respect. Deep down we know when we have lied. However, times come when external pressures push us to be deceptive. That's how it will be for the last generation on Earth.

Prior to the return of Jesus Christ, many catastrophes will strike and believers will be persecuted like never before.[1] In those final days, a worldwide government will order everyone to be marked with a symbol, called the Mark of the Beast. Some people speculate that this mark will be a computer chip embedded under the skin. Taking a more traditional position, others foresee this as an actual mark on a person's forehead. Whatever the form of the mark, people without it will not be able to buy or sell;[2] however, taking the mark has a cost. The Bible is clear: Everybody who accepts it will be excluded from God's family.[3] Just to survive, Christians will be tempted to be dishonest about their faith.

Peter faced a similar quandary. The Pharisees didn't like his preaching and threatened to throw him in jail if he didn't shut up. He told them no[4] and kept preaching. Why did Peter violate existing law? For the greater good of all, he had to conform to the higher laws of God. We can call this a just cause.

What does this have to do with honesty? Basic truth telling is vital to success. Without it, the Pyramid cannot stand upright. However, when we look deeper into this quality we find the need to be honest with God and honest with ourselves in all circumstances, no matter the cost. Coach Wooden had to make a just-cause decision when his player was in jail. The consequences could have been great. Peter broke the law for a just cause and went to jail.

At some point, each of us may need to make a similar just-cause decision. There are powerful forces attempting to remove God from the fabric of our society. The day may come when we must decide whether we will follow a law of the land or the Law of God. Our honesty may be tested.

YOUR TURN

■ **Today's reading:** Acts 2:1-41; 4:1-22; Matthew 28:19-20; John 20:21

1. Think about the last time you were tempted to cheat. What were the circumstances? Did you try to justify it? Did you dwell on the temptation or chase it away? Why did you react the way you reacted? Do you need to change the way you deal with the temptation to cheat?

2. What would you do if faced with a just-cause decision today? What are some situations in which you could break a rule and live with the consequences? What does being honest with yourself and honest with God mean in your life?

❑ I commit myself to being honest with others, with myself and with God.

> *Almighty God, give me the courage to stand up for You even*
> *if there comes a time when the laws of the land say I can't.*
> *I want to be honest with You and true to myself. Through*
> *the power of Your Holy Spirit help me to stay faithful,*
> *even in the face of persecution. Thank You.*

RESOURCEFULNESS

(proper judgment)

WOODEN

Resourcefulness is using our wits, proper judgment and common sense to solve problems and meet challenges. It is using initiative in difficult situations and involves inventing, creating, imagining, synthesizing, evaluating, classifying, observing and analyzing solutions to overcome the trials that life throws at us. Resourcefulness is dreaming up ways to meet our goals.

Some of my greatest pleasures have come from finding ways to overcome obstacles, especially for worthwhile purposes. One of the most resourceful times of my life came while I was at Indiana State, where I wore way too many hats. I was the athletic director, head basketball coach, head baseball coach, teacher and graduate student, all at the same time. There were times when I felt like a plate spinner on the old Ed Sullivan show. He worked real hard keeping all those plates on those sticks. I did too. If I wanted to get anything done, I needed to be resourceful.

That was not the first time I needed to tap resourcefulness. When I was a student and athlete at Purdue University, I had to be resourceful. I needed money; so, I walked the aisle selling sandwiches, candy bars and fruit on the train going to the Purdue-Chicago football games. I even made lapel pins and sold them, but mostly to band members. My last two years at Purdue, I had basketball programs printed and had people sell them at our home games. Today they would call that an entrepreneurial spirit. I just call it resourcefulness.

I had the ambition and desire to be a good student, because making the honor roll gained me a scholarship. I started out studying at night, but everyone else was studying then and there was so much movement and people wanting to chat and socialize that I started going to bed early in the evening and getting up very early in the morning to study. With no interruptions, I got a lot more done in much less time. I could accomplish in two or three hours what previously took four or five, plus I got more sleep. That was a helpful and, I guess, resourceful decision.

I look back on it now and I wonder how I did it. I guess I know. Some of the things I did didn't get done very well. But that doesn't mean I wasn't successful. Actually, it was one of the most successful times of my life. I was making the effort to do my best. Remember, results aren't the criteria for success—it's the effort made for achievement that is most important.

When I arrived at UCLA, I thought I was on vacation. All I had to do was coach basketball. During my Bruin years, my most resourceful times came during the off-season when I would study various aspects of the game in depth and prepare for the next season. Those exercises helped me become a student of the game.

So I tell you, keep on asking, and you will be given what you ask for. Keep on looking, and you will find. Keep on knocking, and the door will be opened (Luke 11:9).

CARTY

Coach Wooden defines resourcefulness as using your wits, proper judgment and common sense to solve problems and meet challenges. By that definition, many biblical characters can be defined as highly resourceful. David is one.

We know David as the slayer of Goliath, the perpetrator of the Bathsheba mess, and ultimately becoming a man after God's own heart. We don't think of him as crazy, but there was a time when he passed himself off as being one wheel short of a rolling chariot.

Before David became king, he needed to learn a bit more about humility. The lesson came when he hid from Saul and ran to King

RESOURCEFULNES

Achish. He thought he was escaping his troubles, but he had only succeeded in going from the proverbial frying pan into the fire. Fortunately for David, he was quick on his feet and decided to fake being nuts. To punctuate his claim of insanity, he scratched on doors and drooled down his beard.[1] Achish fell for the ploy and let David go. As resourceful as David was, his actions were child's play compared to what the virtuous woman of Proverbs 31 was able to accomplish.

The Proverbs 31 woman was so remarkable and accomplished that her man is known simply as Mrs. Amazing's husband. This woman not only took care of her family, but she was also a soft-spoken businesswoman and a stylish artisan who took time to care for the poor and the needy. Her resourcefulness earned her husband's praise: "There are many virtuous and capable women in the world, but you surpass them all!" (Proverbs 31:29).

David and the virtuous woman are examples of people who used resourcefulness to push though challenges. As was true for them, our wits, judgment and common sense will solve many problems. Add prayer and the help of the Holy Spirit to the mix and none of the issues of life need to get the best of us.

I have a favorite saying: *We get what we need when we need it—when we ask for it.* When our will matches God's will and we ask for help, we get what we need.[2] The secret is to match our will with God's will. That occurs when we move closer to God.

The Lord says, "I will guide you along the best pathway for your life. I will advise you and watch over you" (Psalm 32:8). God guides through His Holy Spirit, and that is the best resource of all.

When I get stuck on a problem, I first make sure that my sin is confessed. That aligns me with God. Next I review the situation, pray and go to bed. When I wake up the next morning, an insight is often there. Given a little more time, my wits tempered with sound judgment and common sense, the guidance of the Holy Spirit and prayer, a solution usually comes.

God will never let us be challenged without giving us the tools we need to do the job or solve the problem. We may have to scramble to put those tools to work, but that's where resourcefulness comes in.

YOUR TURN

■ **Today's reading:** 1 Samuel 21:10—22:2; Proverbs 31:10-31; Psalm 32:8; Luke 11:5-13; John 14:12-18

1. Sometimes creative or unconventional approaches are needed. Can you remember an incident when you used creative or unconventional thinking to solve a problem? What was the key to finding the solution?

2. Can you remember a time when prayer and the leading of the Holy Spirit clearly provided an answer to a problem?

❏ I commit myself to using all of the resources God has given me so that creative solutions can be found for the problems I face.

Dear Creator of all Resources, I desire to put all that
You have given me to work for Your honor and glory.
Help me to rely on You for solutions to all the problems
and challenges of life. Teach me to pray and follow the leading
of Your Spirit. Thank You for Your guidance. Amen.

RELIABILITY

(creates respect)

WOODEN

When we are reliable, others know that they can depend on us. They know that we will make the effort to do our best, whatever the situation might be. They know we won't run, cower or become paralyzed by fear. They have learned to count on our consistency and trustworthiness. We'll still be there making the effort to do our best long after the weaker ones have faded. People can bet the farm on us and still be able to sleep at night. Reliability earns the respect of those around us.

Capability doesn't have anything to do with reliability. Some people don't have as much capability as others have, but they make up for their lack by being reliable. Mark Madsen comes to mind. He isn't as capable as many NBA players, but he gets closer to giving you all he has to give more consistently than most of his contemporaries. The coach and his teammates both know what to expect from him every night. He is reliable even though he isn't as capable as some; therefore, his reliability makes him valuable to his team.

Curtis Rowe was one of my most consistent players. Although he wasn't usually spectacular, he consistently played at a very high level and made it look easy. I could have almost penciled in his stat line before the game began. It was a rarity for him not to perform well. I came to count on him. Curtis was as reliable a player as I ever had the privilege to teach.

One of my most reliable players was also versatile. Kenny Heitz was an underrated player, especially when compared to the others on the team at that time. Lew Alcindor, Lucius Allen, Mike Warren and Lynn Shackelford got most of the media attention and Kenny was overlooked. Yet he played in three national championship games and capably filled a different position each year! One year he was a forward and started every game. The next year he was a substitute at both forward and guard. The third year he was my starting guard. How is that for reliability?

Finally, two of my best players during the mid-1950s stood out for different reasons. Morrie Taft was spectacular and explosive. But I never knew how he was going to play from night to night. On the other hand, I knew what Dick "Skeets" Banton would deliver each game. Morrie might get five rebounds, but they were memorable. Dick would get eight or nine, but no one gave them much notice. Most people would say Taft was a better player than Blanton, because Taft had more natural ability and was so dazzling. But I'm not so sure that Skeets wasn't the more valuable player, because of his reliability.

> So Achish called David and said to him, "As surely as the LORD lives, you have been reliable, and I would be pleased to have you serve with me in the army" (1 Samuel 29:6).

CARTY

Barnabas was a reliable member of the New Testament team both as a prophet and as an apostle.[1] He wasn't flashy, but he made those around him better. His name means "son of encouragement." As a discipler, he consistently and reliably lived up to his name. If someone needed salvaging, Barnabas was on it. You could bet the farm on them. He was Mister Reliable, and it didn't matter who got the credit for success. Barnabas specialized in underdogs. He seemed to relish restoring potentially high-powered believers, and he didn't mind when his "projects" went on to rise above him in notoriety or influence.

Barnabas's first major project was Saul, who would become known as the apostle Paul. His second was John Mark, who would write a book of the Bible. Some Christians shoot wounded eagles, but Barnabas would bind their hurts and help them to soar.

Saul was the dreaded nemesis of the faith. He killed as many Christians as he could and was feared. Then he turned to God. Many believers were skeptical regarding Paul's conversion.[2] Not Barnabas. Mr. Reliable went to see Paul, hung out at Starbucks with him, got a sense of his potential and brought him back to the church at Antioch. Barnabas discipled Paul for a year, then set him loose to become arguably the most famous apostle. That was fine with Barnabas. By the time the two men were charged to take money to the famine-stricken poor in Jerusalem, it was Paul who directed the trip.

Paul and Barnabas went on the first missionary journey. They chose John Mark to accompany them, but the younger man bailed at the first sign of trouble. Three years later, as they prepared for the second missionary journey, Barnabas wanted to take John Mark. Paul wouldn't take the risk. Barnabas cared more about John Mark than the mission. As a result, Paul took Silas, went to Asia Minor and changed the world. Barnabas took John Mark, went to Cyprus and changed John Mark. After that, Barnabas isn't mentioned again. Tradition has him being martyred in Cyprus.

The story of Barnabas and John Mark illustrates the two opposite extremes of reliability. Barnabas was strong and dependable. John Mark was fickle and fly-by-night. But thanks to Barnabas, John Mark became so reliable that he served as an evangelist and was given the responsibility of writing a book in the Bible.

It was Barnabas who salvaged John Mark. Mister Reliable invested the latter part of his life into a loser in whom he saw the potential of greatness. Barnabas became a nobody to make another nobody a somebody. Whether God calls you to discipleship (like Barnabas), missions (like Paul), or evangelism (like John Mark), can He pencil in your stats ahead of time? Can you be relied upon to do your part to fulfill your calling, including backing out of the spotlight if it is required?

YOUR TURN

■ **Today's reading:** Acts 9:19-31; 13:1-13; 15:36-40; 2 Timothy 4:9

1. Among the people you know, who are the most dependable ones? Why do you consider them to be reliable?

2. List some of the ways people depend on you. Are you more (or less) dependable now than in the past? How can you become a more reliable person?

❑ I commit myself to keeping my word and to being there for others when they most need help.

Almighty Father, thank You that You are in the business of rescuing the wounded. Bind my hurts, heal me and direct me to the ministry You have planned for me. I want to be Your reliable servant, for Jesus' sake. I want You to be able to pencil in my stats ahead of time. Amen.

RELIABILITY

FIGHT

(determined effort)

WOODEN

Fight is a determined effort to do the very best we can do. On the basketball court, fight is measured by hustle: diving to the floor for loose balls, sprinting to fill a lane on a fast break, taking a charge, picking up a missed defensive assignment, or stealing the ball from an opposing player. It's digging in, gritting our teeth, standing our ground.

When we have fight, we are always ready to respond. We are quick but we don't hurry. We make fewer mistakes because we have the level of our intensity under control. A player with fight has a contained fire burning in his or her belly. This emerges as focused passion. Players with fight never lose a game; they just run out of time.

It's important to know the difference between *being hurt* and *being injured*. People with fight will play with pain, which is okay. Sometimes they will play with an injury, which is not—that can cause further injury. A coach may need to rein back a player who plays when he or she should not.

Nowadays many young people have never experienced fight—they have never worked hard enough to even get their second wind. Too many of today's players don't realize that a bruise or two need not put them out of a game. Hurts and scrapes never stop a person with fight. Only real injuries do that.

These days, I hear a lot of talk about "getting up for a big game." No game should be any bigger than any other. People with fight can't get up any higher for an important game because they get up for every game. When people with fight step onto the floor they always give everything they have to give, whether it's for a practice, a scrimmage or a championship game.

Perhaps I should have chosen a different word. Fight has some negative connotations that I don't want to communicate. In no way is this mortar quality about an opponent. There was a time when I would talk about "being better than the opponent." I don't anymore. Make no mistake; I always want to win, but I never fight with an opponent. My fight is within me—it is the struggle to be the best I can be at whatever I do. This approach works in basketball. If both teams play up to their potential—although only one will take home the prize—both will be winners.

While working on this book, Jay challenged me: "It's hard to get 'win' out of the equation," he said. "To have a winner somebody's got to lose; therefore, winning has to be at somebody else's expense." I understand, but I still feel that no one loses if everyone makes the effort to do his or her best. That's what I've always tried to teach. There's no such thing as losing when we've made the effort to do the best we can do. If we use our fight and determination to do our best, success will take care of itself.

I have fought the good fight, I have finished the race, I have kept the faith (2 Timothy 4:7).

CARTY

Rafer Johnson and C. K. Yang knew how to fight right. They were friends at UCLA and decathlon training partners. While preparing for the 1960 Summer Olympics, Yang noticed a mistake Johnson made repeatedly and suggested that his fellow decathlete adjust his technique. Johnson took Yang's advice and then took the Olympic gold. Yang placed second and received the silver medal. When questioned about having helped the man who would defeat him, Yang was resolute. He only wanted the gold if he was better than Johnson, but he wouldn't know the true outcome unless Johnson was also competing at his best. Both men were winners, even though only one wore the gold.

Paul also knew how to fight right, even if the prize was being stoned (stoned in a biblical sense, *not in a partying sense!*).[1] The apostle and his band of renowned evangelists had been preaching the gospel to the locals in Iconium (a lovely place to flex one's fight!). This motley crew, however, found trouble when some naysayers took offense to the message about a Messiah. Paul and his boys fled Iconium, heading off to Lystra. An angry mob of locals followed, just a few days behind.

The destination of Lystra was precarious at best, for the place had a reputation. According to folklore, generations before Paul turned up in town, the denizens had attempted to boot two other travelers—the Greeks had called the two Zeus and Hermes. Zeus and Hermes knew how to fight—*the wrong way*. Before leaving Lystra, they killed almost all of the townsfolk. The few survivors built a pagan temple and staffed it with a pagan priest, just in case the Greek gods (Zeus and Hermes) ever came back.

Into this milieu blazed Paul and his gang, which included Barnabas. On a bridge just outside Lystra, Paul healed a lame man who jumped up and raced all over town telling everyone what had happened.

Barnabas was tall and good looking—just like Zeus! Paul was quite the orator—just like Hermes! When the townspeople saw Barnabas and heard Paul, they thought Zeus and Hermes had returned, and they tried to worship them. Paul and Barnabas, however, tried to straighten the record and told them about Jesus—*then the troublemakers from Iconium arrived.* The Iconiumers wanted to fight, the wrong way. They stoned Paul, the biblical way.

The fashion of the day was to drag a body that's been stoned out of town, where wild dogs would finish the job. Paul had a different idea, because he had a different definition of fight. He dug deep inside and found the energy to walk back to town, where he spent the night. The next day he started the next leg of his missionary journey—a 60-mile trek to Derbe.

Fourteen years later, Paul wrote about the experience.[2] He was almost certain that he had died, seen heaven and been healed. Whatever happened, I'm sure that after being stoned, it took everything he had to take that first step toward Derbe. Nothing, not even being the object of the wrong kind of fight, could keep Paul from giving his absolute best effort for the cause of Christ. He was determined, and He knew how to fight the good fight.

YOUR TURN

■ **Today's reading:** Acts 14:8-20; 1 Corinthians 12:2-10

1. Describe a time in your life when you fought a good fight but came in second. How were you a winner in that situation?

2. Describe a time in your life when a situation forced you to dig deeper within yourself than you knew you could dig. What did you discover about determination? What does this have to do with knowing how to fight what 2 Timothy 4:7 calls "the good fight"?

❑ I commit myself to fighting the good fight, finishing the race and keeping the faith.

Heavenly Father, I want to give You the best effort of which I am capable of giving. I want to worship You with all of my heart. I want to represent You with all of the zeal of which I am capable. Help me to fight the good fight. Thank You.

INTEGRITY

(purity of intention)

WOODEN

Integrity in its simplest form is purity of intention. It's keeping a clean conscience. But it is also a composite of some of the other mortar qualities in the Pyramid. To some extent, integrity contains a bit of reliability, a healthy helping of honesty and a portion of sincerity. However, I believe that the component of purity of intention is important enough to give integrity the status of mortar in its own right.

Purity of intention is really a reflection of the heart, and having a pure heart is so important that I place it near the top of the Pyramid, just under patience. The heart of a person with integrity always wants to do what's right, once he or she is sure what "right" is.

The Lord created each of us to be unique, and because of that, many of us have differing values. But I believe God put some absolutes in place. The Ten Commandments reflect some of His absolutes. When we violate those absolutes, we fail as people of integrity. Being true to ourselves doesn't make us people of integrity. Charles Manson was true to himself, and as a result, he rightly is spending the rest of his life in prison. Ultimately, being true to our Creator gives us the purest form of integrity.

I wanted my players to become men of integrity. When we have integrity, we are not going to do anything that will be demeaning to anybody else, either on or off the court. And with integrity, we will never consider letting our teammates down. I think I can safely say that the more the quality of integrity was represented in the best seven or eight players on each of my teams, the better their team play became. Great individuals who lack integrity don't usually form great teams, but there are exceptions.

I have had very good basketball players who were not all I wanted them to be off the court. They had what I call "selective integrity." In basketball situations, I could count on them. They were reliable teammates and they were sincerely committed to the team. Some were even on my NCAA championship teams, but they were not successful in my way of thinking. They could have been better. Their selective integrity kept them from becoming all they were capable of becoming.

The five people who first come to mind that best reflect the quality of integrity are Jesus, my dad, Abraham Lincoln, Mother Teresa and Billy Graham. The order of the last three really doesn't matter.

One of the common threads between these people is that each was genuinely concerned about the betterment of others—and Dr. Graham still is. The critics of each might not agree, but in my mind, the integrity of their commitments to regard others as more important than themselves sets them apart. Mother Teresa has been quoted as saying, "A life not lived for others is not a life."[1]

> There was a man named Job who lived in the land of Uz. He was blameless, a man of complete integrity. He feared God and stayed away from evil (Job 1:1).

CARTY

The top five on God's integrity list are Jesus, John the Baptist, Noah, Daniel and Job. You're wondering how I know. The Bible tells us so.

Jesus is the obvious choice for number one. He's perfect and never sinned. I didn't use Christ as an example for any of the other blocks or any of the other mortar qualities, even though He qualifies for each one. It would be the same with gifts and talents. He's got all of them! But since Coach gave us his list, I thought it would be fun to give you God's list, and Jesus is on top.

INTEGRITY

The hearers of Jesus saw actions and words come together. He was credible.[2] Jesus had perfect integrity because there was absolutely no disparity between what He said and what He did.

John the Baptist is second only to Jesus. Jesus called him the greatest person ever born.[3] Since Jesus said it, there can be no argument.

It was God who took the guesswork out of the next three. They are Noah, Daniel and Job, the three most righteous Old Testament saints.[4] Noah is my favorite.

Pause for a moment and think what life would be like for you if you were the only Christian in the world. The pressure to compromise would be intense, wouldn't it? Noah may be the most courageous person who ever lived. People who hate God will hate anyone who represents Him. In Noah's day, everyone but Noah hated God. Noah loved God and stood up for Him. That means Noah was standing alone going toe to toe against the whole world. Through it all, God said Noah was blameless.[5]

Don't mistake blameless for sinless. Everyone has sinned.[6] "Blameless" means "complete and sound." Call it an integrity meter. Noah's love and commitment to God was complete and sound. Sure, Noah sinned, but he never turned his back on God and his words must have matched his actions. Like Abraham, Noah loved God, acted like he loved God and was considered blameless.[7]

It was the same with Daniel. As a young man he chose not to defile himself[8] and went against the orders of the king. Daniel's decision to remain undefiled was the decision of a man with integrity.

Then there was Job. He lived in the land of Uz and was said to be blameless, a man of complete integrity.[9] He feared God and avoided evil. Job embodied integrity.

Where does Mary, the mother of Jesus, fit in the list? We know that she was blessed above all women,[10] but even Jesus didn't rank her above John the Baptist. Since the Bible is silent on how she stacks up against the Old Testament men of integrity, I will slide her in at number three. I know—that puts six people on a list of five. Whoever said basketball players could count? Besides, like Coach's list, the order of the final three (uh, four) on my list does not really matter.

Where you fit doesn't matter either. When it comes to having integrity, God does not keep a top-five list. What matters most are the core commitments that define you as a person. Are you pure in your intentions? Is there consistency between your words and actions, thoughts and choices, values and behaviors? Are you a person of integrity?

YOUR TURN

■ **Today's reading:** Matthew 11:11; 22:16; Ezekiel 14:14; Genesis 6:8-9; Romans 3:21-26; 4:3; Daniel 1:8-16; Job 1:1; Luke 1:39-55

1. Who are the top five people of integrity that you know? Why have you put each on the list?

2. Would any of your friends put you on their top-five list? What do you need to do to increase the purity of intention in your life?

❑ I commit myself to becoming a better representative of Jesus Christ.

Gracious God of Purity, I want my intentions to be pure and my actions to be consistent with my core value of bringing glory to Your holy Name. I want to be a person of impeccable integrity. Guard me against compromise. May there be absolutely no disparity between what I say and what I do. Amen.

PATIENCE

(good things take time)

WOODEN

Patience is the ability to wait and calmly persevere. We all grow impatient, but some people have more trouble waiting than others do. We tend to forget that all good things take time.

Think about the fun of Christmas. Why can't children get to sleep on Christmas Eve? Anticipation! The waiting heightens the joy everyone experiences the next morning. Consider childbirth. We get nine months to anticipate the arrival of a newborn. The mother has to endure the last two months, but the travail makes the prize better. Ponder the harvest. I grew up on a farm. We learned that there was a season to plant, a season to water and a season to harvest. The planting and watering could be laborious, but without those stages there would never be a harvest.

Often the element of time adds value to an accomplishment. Good things take time, as they should. We shouldn't expect good things to happen overnight. Actually, getting something too easily or too soon can cheapen the outcome. For example, people who inherit a lot of money frequently don't appreciate or cannot handle its value. Many end up divorced, broke and disillusioned.

Youth can be impatient. Young people have a tendency to want to change more things more quickly. The mistake they make is that they see all change as progress, and they fail to see the benefit of waiting.

In general, I think we tend to get more patient as we grow older. We don't ruffle as easily. Things don't seem to be as urgent. But older people tend to forget that there is no progress without change. Any organization that isn't moving forward is actually going backward. It is impossible to maintain the status quo; therefore, change is inevitable. The issue is how fast should it come?

Major league baseball teams understand the amount of time and patience needed to produce big-league players. Most of the good ones spend years coming up through the minor league system. This principle of paying your dues is not only found in baseball, but it's also part of the business world, the educational system and most other areas of life. Before success comes patience.

When I came to Los Angeles I was led to believe, but not promised, that my team would have a new arena by the end of my third year. I was shown plans, but it was not built until my eighteenth season. We finally had a home court, and for my last ten years at UCLA we played in Pauley Pavilion. At times my patience was severely tested, but in the end, I was glad that I had waited.

The maxim "easy come, easy go" carries more truth in it than most people realize. When we add to our accomplishments the element of hard work over a long period of time, we'll place a far greater value on the outcome. When we are patient, we'll have a greater appreciation of our success.

Don't you realize how kind, tolerant, and patient God is with you? Or don't you care? Can't you see how kind he has been in giving you time to turn from your sin? (Romans 2:4).

CARTY

Three stories in the Gospel of Luke have a similar theme: God is patient.

The first one is about a man who had one hundred sheep.[1] One day one in the flock wandered away and this shepherd had to go on a search-and-rescue mission.

I never have understood why a responsible shepherd would put an entire flock at risk for one not-so-bright animal. Rustlers, coyotes and wolves could have a field day with the unattended flock. Maybe the stray would wander back on its own. Why gamble? The downside risk was too great for such a small upside potential. At least the shepherd still had 99 sheep. That's the way I saw the situation. But that's not the way God saw it. The 99 sheep represent those who believe in the one true God. What's the worst thing that could happen to them? They could be killed. What happens to them when they are dead? They go to heaven. This does not trivialize life or death; rather, it reveals God's patience.

The apostle Paul explained:

> For to me, living is for Christ, and dying is even better. Yet if I live, that means fruitful service for Christ. I really don't know which is better. I'm torn between two desires: Sometimes I want to live, and sometimes I long to go and be with Christ. That would be far better for me, but it is better for you that I live (Philippians 1:21-26).

The greatest concern, therefore, is for the lost one, not for the 99 that are safe. God specializes in lost sheep. He is patient in the task of finding them. Peter wrote about God's patience:

> The Lord isn't really being slow about his promise to return, as some people think. No, he is being patient for your sake. He does not want anyone to perish, so he is giving more time for everyone to repent (1 Peter 3:9).

That's good news for lost sheep.

The second story is about a woman who lost one of ten valuable coins she owned.[2] She swept every nook and cranny in her house. She lit every corner. She didn't give up. She patiently looked for the coin until she found it. When her patience and perseverance paid off, she ran to her friends. Jesus declared, "In the same way, there is joy in the presence of God's angels when even one sinner repents" (Luke 15:10). That's good news for lost coins.

Finally, we consider the Prodigal Son.[3] A young man talked his dad into giving him an early inheritance; then he ran off, squandered the money, almost starved to death, lived with pigs, and finally decided to return home to see if his dad would accept him as a hired hand.

We don't know how long the Prodigal Son was gone. It was at least several months, perhaps several years. What I love about the story is that from a distance, the dad saw his son coming home. All the time the son was away, the dad had been patiently looking.[4] Likewise, our Father in heaven watches and waits. That's good news if you've been away for a while.

It doesn't matter if you've wandered away, if you've been lost, or if you've squandered your inheritance. Your Heavenly Father has been patiently waiting to welcome you home. Will you come?

YOUR TURN

■ **Today's reading:** Luke 15:4-32; Romans 2:4

1. Are you patient or do you want things to change quickly? Has your patience increased as you have grown older? Give an example of something you now wait to see happen that you might have been impatient to see happen when you were younger.

2. How has God shown His patience with you?

❏ I commit to learn how to wait without being anxious. I want to learn patience.

Patient Father, thank You for never giving up on me. I want to come home and feel Your welcoming embrace. Amen.

FAITH

(through prayer)

WOODEN

I believe that we must have faith that things are going to turn out as they should. That doesn't necessarily mean that they're going to turn out as we would want them to turn out; nevertheless, we must have faith that they will. For this to happen, we must do our part to help our faith become reality. This is faith in ourselves, but it is also a faith in something or someone greater than ourselves.

God is either in control or He isn't. I believe He is. But I also believe that He delegates certain responsibilities to us. This does not mean that we earn His favor. We can't work our way into His good graces. But we do have some responsibility in the successful development of our faith. Faith without works is dead. Likewise, works without faith are also worthless.[1]

My dad encouraged me to build a shelter for a rainy day. He wasn't hinting that I should build a home on Earth. He was talking about faith. Specifically he wanted me to trust God to prepare a home for me after this life is over. I have tried to do my part in building this shelter. I've trusted Christ and I've tried to live as He would have me live. I've studied His Word and I've prayed a great deal. I have faith that He will do what He's promised. I'm ready to meet Him and I'm eager to see my wife, Nellie; but all in due time. I don't want to outlive my children or my grandchildren, but neither am I ready to leave my family. Actually, I've put the timing into God's hands. As He would have it, we lost my son-in-law, Dick, the Sunday before Christmas 2004.

I served as a basketball coach at a public institution; therefore, I didn't talk about my faith. I never felt it was appropriate. I always had a Bible on my desk and I intentionally led by example, based on

Christ's teaching; but I wasn't vocal about my beliefs. I just attempted to demonstrate them by the way I live my life.

Some evangelical Christians think of me as being liberal because they disagree with my decision to let my life speak for my faith. At the same time, liberals consider me to be way too conservative. I know you can't please everyone, so on this issue I haven't tried. I have only wanted to please God.

In its purest form, faith in God wasn't a part of my curriculum, so I didn't preach. I'm not a minister in that sense. I was a basketball coach who was charged with producing good men and graduates who also played basketball.

It was important to me to never come across as being critical of someone else's faith. It never bothered me if someone believed differently, and I understood that some of them were just as set in their faith as I am in mine. As a result, I never tried to change a person's faith. I saw that as God's job, not mine. I did encourage my players to have a faith and to be able to defend it, but also to stay open-minded. I felt that those who were open-minded would give way to truth and those who weren't wouldn't. I have always believed that what Christ said is truth, and that He is Truth.

> Therefore, since we have been made right in God's sight by faith, we have peace with God because of what Jesus Christ our Lord has done for us (Romans 5:1).

CARTY

There was a time when people could hold whatever values they chose to hold without needing the endorsement of others. Tolerance was considered to be consent without approval. We had the right to opine that other people were wrong without denying their right to live as they chose to live. That was called freedom of choice. But times have changed. Today's definition of tolerance requires both

FAITH

consent and approval of any values or behavior of others, even if we object or feel that God disapproves.

When it came to spiritual matters, there was a time when people could follow whichever god they chose to follow, but we had the right to assert that they were wrong. Our convictions didn't give us the right to persecute others, but we did have the right to disagree without being juxtaposed as enemies.

Today's mind shapers would have us believe that any serious seeker will find a path to God because all faiths are the same. Moreover, anyone who does not fall in line with this thinking is judged to be a judgmental bigot. In basketball, we would call that new-school thinking.

Coach and I are old school. We still believe that people have the right to believe that others are wrong, and that such disagreements shouldn't hurt our relationships. It is important to explain how the concept of tolerance has changed because of faith being an integral part of the apex of the Pyramid of Success.

It has been Coach Wooden's observation that players who have faith are generally more consistent in making the effort to become the best they can be than those who do not have faith. That works well on the basketball floor and in the boardroom, but there is a bigger question about faith.

The Pyramid helps us become successful with life's endeavors, no matter our faith—as long as we have one. But the fruit of our lives won't solve the problem that occurs at life's end. I believe there will be good people who do not go to heaven because they didn't get the faith part right.

There are Hindus, Buddhists, Muslims, Taoists, Sikhs, animists, Scientologists, and so many more. The world is full of religions that claim to be the best or only way; however, they can't all be correct. Jesus said, "I am the way, the truth, and the life. No one can come to the Father except through me" (John 14:6).

If Jesus is wrong, then all the good people in the world, no mat-

FAITH

ter their faith, are possibly on the right path. On the other hand, if He is right, everyone who doesn't know Him will end up separated from God, no matter how successful they are in life.[2] Those who miss heaven can hardly be considered a success. The issue of eternity makes faith the most important principle in the Pyramid of Success.[3]

YOUR TURN

■ **Today's reading:** John 14:1-12; Romans 3:21-28; 5:1-11; James 2:14-26; 2 Thessalonians 1:3-12

1. Coach encouraged his players to have a faith and to be able to defend it. In what do you have faith and how do you defend it?

2. If Jesus truly is the only way, how does this affect your perception of faith and its place in the Pyramid? How can you better work out this faith in your life?

❏ I commit to study the claims of Jesus Christ. I want to know if He really is the only way to God.

Dear God and Father of Faith, I want to get this right. I want Jesus Christ to be my Lord and Savior. Amen.

SUCCESS

Success is peace of mind that is a direct result of self-satisfaction in knowing you did your best to become the best you are capable of becoming.

WOODEN

When do we know that we have succeeded?

When asking ourselves this question, we should forget what others think. They don't know. We should be more concerned with our character than with our reputation: Our character is what we truly are, while our reputation is merely what others perceive us to be. As I have often said, having a good reputation doesn't determine success. Neither do awards, accolades or achievements.

Winning seems so important, but it actually is irrelevant. Having attempted to give our all is what matters—and we are the only ones who really know the truth about our own capabilities and performance. Did we do our best at this point in our life? Did we leave all we had to give on the field, in the classroom, at the office or in the trenches? If we did, then we are a success—at that stage of our life. But being successful at one point doesn't necessarily make us a success at every point—and it does not mean that we reach the apex. We must learn to give our all in one success after another. Likewise, accomplishing certain goals does not necessarily translate to success.

As I write these words, I am 94 years old. God has given me good health beyond what most people could ever dream to have. I still drive my car for short distances. I am still independent, and I want to stay that way. I want to continue to live in the home that I shared with my dear wife, Nellie. But being able to accomplish that goal has nothing to do with being successful. Goals are wonderful in that they stretch us and help us reach our potential, but making or missing goals has nothing to do with success.

It is not my way to count or list my awards. The publisher might include them at the back of this book, but I didn't ask for them to be there. I know that people still want to hear me speak, and I am honored by their requests. People still want to meet with me—in fact, they come from all over the world. It is a privilege to be able to continue to encourage others. My hectic schedule has probably done much to keep my mind as clear as it is, even though it's not as sharp as it once was. My family has been around me, too. What a blessing that has been! I am blessed beyond belief—but am I a success?

Believe me when I say, none of these factors is part of the criteria. I am not saying I don't appreciate the blessings that have come my way. I am not saying that at all. But if none of these good things had ever occurred, I would not be any less successful.

I can recount the blessings in my life, but blessings aren't success. The real determining factor is this: Did I make the effort to do my best? That is the only criteria, and I am the only one who knows (well, me and God).

Am I a success?

I have peace of mind.

Well done, my good and faithful servant (Matthew 25:21).

CARTY

Paul was calm as he wrote, even though it would be his last letter. He had peace of mind even though Nero would soon have his head. The apostle was in his early 60s, writing from the Mamertine prison in Rome to his friend and disciple, Timothy. Since Paul wasn't sure when he was going to die, he wanted Timothy to bring him a cloak before winter.[1] When the temperature dropped, it would be cold and damp in his dungeon.

I'm guessing the great apostle called Timothy "Timmy" when they first met, many years earlier. Timmy would become Tim and, finally, Timothy. The changing of names reflects the process of maturation.

Timmy, along with his Grandma Lois and his mom, Eunice, were present the day Paul was stoned in Lystra. That is when Timmy grew to be Tim. Witnessing a friend get stoned matures a lad in a hurry. By the time Paul returned to Lystra three years later—on his second missionary journey—Tim had become known as Timothy, a disciple of Jesus Christ. Seeing how much his friend had matured, Paul invited him to join the tour.

Eventually Timothy became a pastor, but Paul never missed an opportunity to teach and disciple him. The great apostle reminded Timothy to preach persistently, put things right with patience, keep a clear mind, not be afraid of suffering, continue to bring people to Christ and to complete the ministry God had given to him.[2] The apostle even defined success for him:

> As for me, my life has already been poured out as an offering to God. The time of my death is near. I have fought a good fight, I have finished the race, and I have remained faithful. And now the prize awaits me—the crown of righteousness that the Lord, the righteous Judge, will give me on that great day of his return. And the prize is not just for me but for all who eagerly look forward to his glorious return (2 Timothy 4:6-8).

Paul gave his life to God. He gave everything he had to every task. Although he occasionally stumbled, he didn't quit, drop out or give up. His faith never wavered. In every situation, he trusted God, served Christ and finished well. He knew that he would hear God say, "Well done, good and faithful servant." He had peace of mind.

On Earth, success is having peace of mind in knowing that we have done our best to become the best that we are capable of becoming. When we have this peace, we have reached the apex of the Pyramid of Success.

In eternity, success also is having done our best to allow God to do His best in us and through us. When we live like this, we too will hear the words "Well done!" and we too will have a peace that passes all understanding.[3]

YOUR TURN

■ **Today's reading:** 2 Timothy 4:1-22; Matthew 25:14-30; Jeremiah 29:11-13

1. Where are you on Coach Wooden's Pyramid of Success? List the Building Blocks and Mortar Qualities. Write a sentence about each one explaining how it is manifest (or not manifest) in your life. Which ones do you need to work on the most?

2. Looking at your life up to now, using Coach Wooden's definition, are you a success? Why or why not?

3. Do you have the peace that passes all understanding? Will you hear the words "Well done"? What changes can you make in your life so that you can be all that God created you to be?

❑ I commit myself to putting aside selfish goals and to setting new noble goals that will help other people and bring glory to God.

Great God and Author of Plans, thank You for Your plans for
me. I want to live up to my responsibilities in being all that
You created me to be. Grant to me the courage to make the effort
to do my best to become all that I can become to bring glory to
You and advance Your kingdom. Father I long to hear You say,
"Well done, my good and faithful servant." May it be so.

ENDNOTES

Introduction
1. Source unknown.

Building Block 1 (Part 1) (Industriousness)
1. See Acts 8:1-3.
2. See 2 Corinthians 11:23-27.
3. See 1 Corinthians 10:31.

Building Block 1 (Part 2) (Industriousness)
1. John W. Bunn, *Basketball Methods* (New York: Macmillan Company, 1939), n.p.
2. See Psalms 33:11; 40:5; Jeremiah 29:11.
3. See Genesis 11:4-6.
4. See Genesis 41.

Building Block 2 (Enthusiasm)
1. See 1 Corinthians 4:6.

Building Block 3 (Friendship)
1. Swen Nater, "Friendship." Used by permission.
2. See Ruth 1:16.
3. See 1 Samuel 18:3.
4. See Job 2:11.
5. See Daniel 3:27.

Building Block 4 (Cooperation)
1. See Revelation 4:8.
2. See Romans 12:3-8; Ephesians 4:7-16; 1 Corinthians 12:1-11.
3. See 1 Peter 4:10.
4. See 1 Thessalonians 5:19.

Building Block 5 (Loyalty)
1. See 1 Chronicles 11:11.
2. See 1 Chronicles 11:18-19.
3. See Hebrews 13:8; James 1:17.

Building Block 6 (Self-Control)
1. See Genesis 39:2.
2. See Genesis 39:6.
3. Ibid.
4. See Romans 3:23.

Building Block 7 (Alertness)
1. See Judges 7:12.
2. See 1 Peter 5:8, *NASB*.
3. See Ephesians 6:10-20.

Building Block 8 (Initiative)
1. Author unknown.
2. See John 13:21.
3. Philippians 4:6.
4. "Hebrew-Aramaic and Greek Dictionaries," *BibleMaster 3.0.* CD-ROM. The Lockman Foundation, 1981.
5. See Luke 22:44. The clinical term is "hematohidrosis." Stress constricts the network of capillaries around the sweat glands. If for some reason the vessels dilate rapidly, they will rupture, infusing the sweat gland with blood. (Source: Third Day Ministries. http://www.ourchurch.com/view/?pageID=34573 [accessed April 14, 2004].) Whether Jesus sweated like blood or actually sweated blood is irrelevant, either is possible. The point is that it takes great stress and fear to produce either condition.

Building Block 9 (Intentness)
1. See Leviticus 15:25.
2. See Matthew 9:21.
3. Luke 8:45.
4. Luke 8:46.

Building Block 10 (Condition)
1. See 1 Kings 16:29—18:46. (There is more to the story of Elijah but space limitations prohibited covering it all.)
2. See 1 Kings 18:46.
3. Acts 24:16, *KJV*.
4. 1 Timothy 4:8.

Building Block 11 (Skill)
1. See Ephesians 5:16.

2. For a thorough study of this concept, see John Bradley and Jay Carty, *Discovering Your Natural Talents* (Colorado Springs, CO: NavPress, 1994), n.p.

3. See Mark 10:43.

4. See James 4:6.

5. See Matthew 5:19.

6. See Luke 22:26.

7. If you have yet to discover your potential for excellence, read *Discovering Your Natural Talents*. The book contains exercises specifically designed to help you determine your wiring. Also, start praying specifically that God will show you what He wants you to do. The trick to that one is being open to what He shows you and to where He might send you to do it. But rest assured, He wouldn't call you to a task that He hasn't given you the skill to do.

Building Block 12 (Team Spirit)

1. Adapted from *Encyclopedia of 15,000 Illustrations*, #14246.

2. See Romans 12:3.

Building Block 13 (Poise)

1. See Exodus 4:10.

2. See Esther 2:7.

3. See Esther 2:15,17; 5:8.

4. See Leviticus 26:13.

Building Block 14 (Confidence)

1. See Acts 7:2-56.

2. See Acts 6:3.

3. See Acts 6:8.

4. See Acts 6:15.

5. See Acts 7:55.

6. See Acts 7:59.

Building Block 15 (Competitive Greatness)

1. I use the word "superstars" because there are always exceptions. Some people have so much talent that they are just better than anyone else, without giving all they have to give. That might make them superstars, but by my definition it doesn't make them successes.

2. See Ephesians 6:10-17.

Mortar Quality 1 (Ambition)

1. See 2 Samuel 13:1–18:18.
2. See 2 Samuel 2:4; 15:1-6.
3. See James 3:16.

Mortar Quality 2 (Sincerity)
1. See Matthew 14:3-4.
2. See Matthew 14:6-8.
3. See Matthew 11:11.
4. See 1 John 1:9.

Mortar Quality 4 (Honesty)
1. See Revelation 8:1–21:8.
2. See Revelation 13:17.
3. See Revelation 14:11.
4. See Acts 4:19-20.

Mortar Quality 5 (Resourcefulness)
1. See 1 Samuel 21:13.
2. See John 14:14.

Mortar Quality 6 (Reliability)
1. See Acts 13:1; 14:14.
2. See Acts 9:26.

Mortar Quality 7 (Fight)
1. See Acts 14:8-20.
2. See 1 Corinthians 12:2.

Mortar Quality 8 (Integrity)
1. Mother Teresa, source unknown.
2. See Matthew 22:16.
3. See Matthew 11:11.
4. See Ezekiel 14:14.
5. See Genesis 6:9.
6. See Romans 3:23.
7. See Romans 4:3.
8. See Daniel 1:8.
9. See Job 1:1.

10. See Luke 1:42.

Mortar Quality 9 (Patience)

1. See Luke 15:4-7.
2. See Luke 15:8-10.
3. Luke 15:11-32.
4. Luke 15:20.

Mortar Quality 10 (Faith)

1. See James 2:17.
2. 2 Thessalonians 1:8-9.
3. If you don't agree with these statements and if your mind is made up, let's still be friends. But if you are open, and if you would like more information about these concepts, log on to jaycarty.com and order *Playing with Fire*. I'll give it to you free of charge if you'll pay the shipping and handling. Click on "Pyramid Offer."

The Apex (Success)

1. See 2 Timothy 4:22.
2. See 2 Timothy 4:1-5.
3. If you have the assurance that you will hear "Well done," we thank you for reading our book and hope that you have grown in your relationship with God. If you aren't sure, then we invite you to explore more. A good place to start is by reading the Gospels. You will also find information in *Playing with Fire*, a book we offer to you for free (see Mortar Quality 10, endnote 4).

LEARNING FROM THE LEGEND

How Four Former UCLA Players Applied the Pyramid Principles on the Court and in the Ministry

DR. JACK L. ARNOLD
UCLA 1954-1956
PRESIDENT, EQUIPPING PASTORS INTERNATIONAL
WINTER SPRINGS, FLORIDA

John Wooden, an all-American college player, a winning coach with 10 NCAA championships, the most respected coach in college basketball history and the idol and envy of every basketball coach in the world, is a modest man who not only teaches the principles in the Pyramid of Success but also lives by them. The character of John Wooden is found in his own Pyramid.

These building blocks and mortar qualities influenced me as a young man; as a Christian learning and struggling through life (I came to know Christ in my junior year at UCLA); as a pastor teaching and relating to people; and as a missionary seeking to change the world for Christ. The Pyramid of Success hangs in my office and is personally signed by Coach. I regularly look at it to remind me of the things I need to do in order to be successful. The three building blocks that have had the greatest impact on my life are *industriousness*, *initiative* and *team spirit*.

As a pastor and a missionary, I must be *industrious*. While a Christian walks by faith in Christ and in the truths found in the Bible, he or she must also work to demonstrate the reality of that faith. Sometimes this work is hard, demanding and tedious. Also, there must be human planning. While God has a plan known only to Him, He uses our human strategy to bring about His own purposes—a great mystery. John Wooden taught me to work hard, to constantly learn and to never quit. Unfortunately, I did not always take Mr. Wooden's advice! I quit varsity basketball at UCLA my senior year. I had just become a Christian, and everything in life paled into insignificance compared to the new life I found in Christ. However, to this day I regret my decision to give up the sport.

In the difficulties of the ministry, I have been tempted to quit many times; but I have not done so because of God's sustaining grace. Once when I made a mistake on the basketball floor and sulked about it, Coach said, "Goodness gracious, Jack Arnold, stop whining and complaining. Jump up and get into the game. You help no one by pouting over something you cannot change, but you can change the outcome of the game by getting back into it."

The second block that has influenced me greatly is *initiative*. As a minister of the gospel of Christ, I must make major decisions almost daily, and many of these decisions can affect a person's whole life—even influencing one's thinking about his or her eternal destiny.

Sometimes I find myself the only one who feels a certain way, and I often have to stand alone to be true to myself and to my God. There are times that I have made bad decisions and failed, both of which can be used by God in a powerful way. I remember one day when I went to Coach's office to tell him I was quitting basketball. He listened patiently, was very gracious and encouraged me to do whatever God had put on my heart to do. He sensed that whatever decision I made, even if it resulted in failure, would somehow work out for good.

The third block that influenced my life is *team spirit*. When I came to UCLA, I thought I was a hotshot, because in high school I had been named the outstanding CIF player of the year for small schools. Despite the accolade, I had been poorly coached in high school and was very much a non-team player. Coach Wooden taught me the fundamentals of basketball and convinced me that no individual was greater than the team. In fact he deplored the "star" concept and stressed giving up personal interests for the good of the team.

The concept of teamwork really helped me in the ministry. No one can pastor a successful church without each individual member feeling part of the team. The church members find a way to win together as a team when each one contributes to the good of the whole. If they win, they win as a team, giving the glory to God. If they lose, they lose together, asking God how they can improve to win another day.

Behind the character of John Wooden are two basic principles that make him the man that he is. The first is *integrity*. Coach Wooden is a man who can be trusted. He graciously says what he means and means what he says. There is never any doubt about his intentions. Integrity is the sum total of all that we are. While Coach Wooden has his faults (as all people do), his integrity raises him a notch above his peers. That integrity has been an example to me for 45 years as a Christian and 38 years as a minister. I can count on one hand the people who have influenced my life in a big way, and John Wooden is one of them. The other four are ordained ministers. The uniqueness of Coach Wooden is that he is a faithful and steady Christian who walks the walk for Christ without the trappings of professional religion.

The second principle that best characterizes Coach is *faith*. He is a man who reads the Bible and prays, knowing that without these he can do nothing that will count for time or eternity. Coach's life of faith has been an example for me and has challenged me to live the same way.

There is a moral quality to Coach Wooden that is not included in the Pyramid of Success—and that is *humility*. This quality is not mentioned because he is truly a humble man. With all the great achievements and accolades that have come his way, John Wooden knows that all he is, all that he has accomplished and all that he has given to others is because of the grace of God. A humble person is not one who drops his head, stares at the floor and says, "I'm nothing; I'm nobody." A truly humble man knows who he is in Christ, acknowledging all that God has done in, for and through him, and then gives all the glory to God. This, I believe, is the real key to John Wooden's human success.

My favorite photo of Coach Wooden shows him meditating (possibly praying) with his head bowed, his hands crossed and his eyes focused on the pages of a book. It depicts him as reflective, spiritual and humble. This is the John Wooden I most love, respect and admire. I cherish this picture, which he signed: "For Jack Arnold, a fellow Christian and one of my boys. With love, John Wooden, UCLA."

Special Note
Dr. Jack Arnold died on January 9, 2005, while preaching the gospel at his home church in central Florida. Nearing the end of his sermon titled "The Cost of Discipleship," which was based on Luke 14:25-35, Dr. Arnold exhorted the people toward a deeper commitment to Christ—even if it meant dying for Him. Dr. Arnold quoted John Wesley, who had said that believers are immortal until their work for the Kingdom is complete. Then Dr. Arnold said, "I don't know about you, but when my work for Christ is done, I am out of here. I am going to be with Jesus. And that will be great gain." Just a few sentences later, he paused, looked up briefly and fell back, dying from cardiac arrest. Moments before his death, he had also quoted his favorite verse, "For me, to live is Christ, to die is gain" (Philippians 1:21, NASB).

RALPH DROLLINGER
UCLA 1972-1976
MINISTRY LEADER, CAPITOL MINISTRIES
SACRAMENTO, CALIFORNIA

In 1972, my first year at UCLA, freshmen were deemed eligible to play on the varsity team. I therefore found myself practicing with the

Walton gang; and for reasons more to do with timing than ability, I would become the first player to go to the NCAA Final Four Tournament four years in a row. It was during one of those first practices that I learned a huge lesson that I will never forget—a lesson that would shape my life for years to come.

After grabbing a defensive rebound, I turned to make my outlet pass to the awaiting guard near the sideline, just this side of the half court. In an irresponsible fashion I threw away the outlet pass (it was intercepted). Coach Wooden blew his whistle, stopped practice and kindly instructed me in front of my championship-winning teammates, "Ralph, you are not to throw away the outlet pass."

"Yes sir!" I replied, standing somewhat at attention with my tennis shoes properly laced and my jersey neatly tucked into my seemingly tailored all-white, all-cotton practice gear.

About a half hour later, I threw away another outlet pass. This time in stopping the practice, Coach questioned me in a now more distinguishable tone of admonition, "Ralph, do you know why you are not to throw away the outlet pass?" I knew enough to know that this was my clue to briefly recite the philosophy of a fast-break offense and the numerical advantage that is either gained or lost depending on the successful completion of the outlet pass. Coach seemed to buy my respect-laden response, and the balletlike practice continued under the careful, scrutinizing eye of the master choreographer.

Near the end of practice, guess what happened? I threw away another outlet pass. With an unmistakable sense of sternness, Coach thrice blasted his whistle, much like the final, powerful notes of a grand symphony. Coach sat me down on the half-court paint, and with teammates overshadowing the impromptu meeting, he exhorted me with furled brow and pointed finger, "Ralph, if you ever throw away one more outlet pass, you will be denied the privilege of practice with your teammates." I was beginning to get the message.

Coach Wooden's success in the discipline of basketball is often and correctly attributed to his emphasis on the proper execution of the fundamentals. The aforementioned is intended to illustrate just that. Perhaps the greatest legacy of Coach's life will be this constant and unmistakable theme: One positions himself or herself to best serve his Maker and fellow man by inordinately concentrating on the fundamentals of his chosen profession—and working consistently and industriously (the cornerstone of his Pyramid of Success) at the task of proper dispatch, especially when under intense pressure.

Every profession has its inviolate fundamentals that need to be rigorously adhered to. The success of Coach Wooden's career serves to vividly illuminate this important truth. As a matter of fact, 10 national championships in 12 years should serve as underscores and exclamation marks to this insight! Those banners hanging in Pauley Pavilion (UCLA's home arena) lend indisputable testimony to this truth and serve to indelibly etch the incredibly important need for one to major on the fundamentals throughout his or her life and career.

It was during my playing days under Coach Wooden that I sensed a call into the gospel ministry of Jesus Christ, and that has been the professional pursuit of my life since graduating from the Westwood campus in 1976. Accordingly, in my area of vocation, I have sought to apply and execute the basic, often repeated truths of the Bible as I minister to elected officials, staff and lobbyists in the California capitol.

Unfortunately, however, to say in our society that you are a minister who practices the fundamentals of Scripture earns you the label of fundamentalist. In the world of religious understanding, such a label carries derisive overtones and a negative connotation in the minds of many. This is unfortunate for those of us who, like Coach Wooden, labor to emphasize the basics. The term "fundamental," as it is used in Christian circles, dates back to a significant 1910-1912 work called *The Fundamentals*. These volumes summarized basic Christian doctrines found repeatedly in the Scriptures. The publication of these books came in response to the incursion of the Social Gospel movement (which, in a nutshell, sought to remove Christ's deity and revise His ministry emphasis to be one of social change versus individual heart change). *The Fundamentals* was a cogent apologetic, summarizing the essence of true-to-the-Bible ministry.

Unlike a basketball coach, a minister who practices the basics gets tagged with a difficult label in today's society. But most of the time, fundamentalist ministers have as their hearts' objective the desire to remain faithful to the text of Scripture—and its authorial intent. I attribute Coach Wooden's tutoring of me via basketball to having made me into a fundamentalist. And I am proud of that title, because it is only in properly conveying the fundamental nature of the Scripture that will ultimately lead to the best outcome in the heart of a listener.

As I look back over the lives of those whom I have had the blessed opportunity to lead to a saving faith in Christ or to disciple in the truths of Scripture, I am thankful that Coach Wooden modeled and kindled such an emphasis on fundamentals in my heart. Even though Coach might not have bought it back then, God had a reason for my throwing away those outlet passes!

But of even greater importance, it is on the basis of one's faithfulness to the text of Scripture that will determine whether the Master in heaven will state of His follower on the Day of Judgment, "Well done, my good and faithful servant" (Matthew 25:23). Thank you for instilling in me a passion for the fundamentals, Coach; it is one that promises both present and eternal benefits.

DOUG McINTOSH, PH.D.
UCLA 1964-1966
SENIOR PASTOR, CORNERSTONE BIBLE CHURCH
LILBURN, GEORGIA

In the 39 years since I graduated from UCLA, dozens of people have asked me what it was like to play for Coach John Wooden. It is a testimony to how deeply Coach is admired that such a question is so consistently asked, but I have always found it difficult to give a short answer to the question. How do you compress a whole worldview into a few minutes of casual conversation?

I have told people quite often that every UCLA basketball player who spent time under Coach Wooden's tutelage received more than improved skills. He received a way of thinking about solving problems and overcoming obstacles. If you paid attention and believed in what he said, you not only became a better basketball player, you also became a more competent person. He was as much a philosopher as a coach, and he was equally proficient at both activities. My basketball skills I lost long ago, but the life principles he left with me are more valuable today than they were when I first heard them.

A case in point: One of the building blocks of Coach Wooden's Pyramid of Success is self-control—exchanging short-term comforts for long-term excellence. During the years I was at UCLA, we played against many excellent teams, some of which had better athletes. Yet we lost to very few of them, in large measure because we were in better condition than any team we played. By the middle of the second half, we had often worn down opponents with our full-court-pressing defense and fast-break offense.

The price we paid for that advantage was a rigorous practice schedule. When the Los Angeles smog hung in nearly visible brownness in our home arena in October, Coach insisted that we had to push ourselves beyond what we thought we could. The NCAA championship trophies that we received in March had their beginnings in the oxygen-deprived practices of October. It was a valuable lesson that has stayed with me: You can usually do more than you think you can. It takes a good coach to make that lesson penetrate skulls that were inclined toward personal comforts.

Coach believed that you played as you prepared. If you didn't exercise self-control at developing your basketball habits during the week, your inattention to detail would rise up and bite you when game time came. Consequently, our practices were about 70 percent drills. We ran our high-post offense so much that, though I haven't been involved in it in for nearly 40 years, I could diagram the entire system right now without much effort. Coach preached the principle that if you have to think about it, you'll do it too slowly. Developing self-control in doing things the right way every time will give you the ability to, in his words, "execute the fundamentals quickly."

Coach insisted that we concentrate on our own behavior (which we could control) and not focus on what the other team might do. He virtually never showed us scouting reports on our opponents. The only exception I can remember was before a game during my sophomore season, when we went undefeated. Coach handed us each a 30-page printout on our opponents, giving a detailed description of each player. By the time I finished reading the information, I was convinced that we would be fortunate to stay in the game against such a fantastic team. The scout made them sound like a combination of Red Auerbach's Boston Celtics and Phil Jackson's Chicago Bulls. Then the game started, and we were up by 30 at halftime.

They were the worst team we played during my years at UCLA. I guess he figured that we wouldn't take them seriously if we knew of their weaknesses; and he was right—we wouldn't have. More important, he let us know every week that he would judge us not by whether we defeated the other team but by whether we played the way we were capable of playing. We received some of our sternest criticisms after a win, when it was apparent that we were coasting instead of playing the hustling and intelligent game we should have been. Coach, in fact, almost never talked about winning. He did talk a lot about playing up to our potential, and we discovered that doing that is considerably harder than winning.

The importance of holding oneself accountable is a lesson I haven't forgotten. It is not only true in basketball, it is also true in life. Nobody has ever given me half as much grief as I give myself. I find that if I stop blaming other people for my troubles and start

COACH WOODEN'S PYRAMID OF SUCCESS

looking at my own performance, I always end up better off. Coach Wooden wasn't the first person to tell me that, but by the time he said it, I was mature enough to see that he was telling me the truth; and for that, I will be forever grateful.

WILLIE NAULLS
UCLA 1953-1956
PASTOR, WILLIE NAULLS MINISTRIES
LAGUNA NIGUEL, CALIFORNIA

Many years ago, after retiring from professional basketball, I picked up the three Boston Celtics championship rings that I had earned and headed home to Los Angeles. Ten years had passed since I had left UCLA to begin my NBA career. After a few days of adjustment, I called my college coach and asked him for an audience. John Wooden agreed, and several days later I found myself sitting across from him at his desk. As I scanned the walls, I saw photos of past UCLA players and teams.

His Pyramid of Success was prominent and prompted me to ask him a question I had long entertained. Pointing to the top of his Pyramid, I asked, "Do you use the word 'faith' to mean the God-kind of faith, as used in the Bible?" I was hoping for a yes or no answer, but Coach did what he is best at. He responded in a way that would make me work out the answer for myself.

Looking at the top of the Pyramid, he said that his concern was for the development of faith in ourselves. He ended his answer there, but he seemed a bit uneasy. I knew there was more. I realized that he was not suggesting a New Age self-realization philosophy. I also understood his concept of the need to have enough faith in our own abilities to get a job done. But what exactly was the more for which he had left open the door?

A good teacher inspires thought and pursuit of understanding. Coach's answer caused me to pursue the deeper spiritual meaning of the word "faith," which had eluded me until I committed my life to serving in the ministry of Jesus Christ. I learned that Christ Jesus is the gift of faith from God. A personal relationship with Christ Jesus is the only way to know what real faith is. In Scripture, we read that without faith it is impossible to please God (see Hebrews 11:6). I soon discovered that the God-kind of faith is important. We are encouraged by God's Word to know the importance that He places on faith. God's Word gives us the universal truth about faith.

> So whatever you believe about these things [choice of eating habits] keep between yourself and God. Blessed is the man who does not condemn himself by what he approves. But the man who has doubts is condemned if he eats, because his eating is not from faith; and everything that does not come from faith is sin (Romans 14:22-23, *NIV*).

Faith is a private and personal choice, as demonstrated in the life of Coach Wooden. Believing without the physical evidence or materiality of things hoped for is the faith offered in Christ as a virtue—characterized as the fruit of God's Spirit in believers (see Galatians 5:22).

As my coach and wise counselor, Coach Wooden fulfilled his responsibility to inspire me on the subject of faith. I was allowed to make up my mind without the intrusion of his personal spiritual conviction about God. My mom was very specific in her teaching that I needed the God-kind of faith (see Mark 11:22) to survive in a world that looked upon me as a skin color—an adjective, not a noun. Parents have a mandate from God to train up their children in the way they should go (see Proverbs 22:6). Having the God-kind of faith is a virtue I choose to live daily. Coach Wooden encouraged me to develop strong faith in myself even as he lived the God-kind of faith before me. Coach and my mom were role models to be emulated.

Is He Is or Is He Ain't—a Saint?*
By William D. Naulls

I've been asked countless times over the years
Is Coach Wooden a believer?
Or just a modest country-boy overachiever?
Coach's Pyramid of Success devotional is out.
Now all Christian doubters can shout
JOHN ROBERT WOODEN is a believer! And
Christ through him is the Achiever.

* The title of this poem is a play on words based on Louis Jordan's old song "Is You Is or
Is You Ain't My Baby?"

JOHN R. WOODEN

These days John Wooden can be found in the stands at UCLA home basketball games and being interviewed on television during the NCAA basketball playoffs. Each spring he presents the John R. Wooden Award for the collegiate basketball player of the year. And many recognize him as the best college basketball coach ever. Off the court, he spends time with his family, former players and an ever-expanding circle of friends.

Into his nineties, Wooden maintains a busy schedule that includes some personal appearances. Somehow he always has time to meet with a high school coach, sign an autograph or offer a kind word to a fan. In fact, he has such a disciplined regimen that he ably turned around approvals on the edits of the manuscript for this book in half the time authors a third of his age usually take.

John Wooden was born on October 14, 1910, in Martinsville, Indiana, the second of four brothers. Coach Wooden's father, Joshua, instilled in his sons the basic principles of honesty, hard work and respect for others—the elements that make up the Pyramid of Success. He also passed along to them a love for reading, especially the Bible and poetry.

Wooden was the star of the Martinsville High School basketball team, leading the team to the Indiana state championship in 1927. Two other years his team was the runner-up, and three times Wooden was named to the all-state team. At Purdue University, the five-foot-ten guard was a three-time All-American, but he is most proud of being an Academic All-American. In 1932, he scored about a third of his team's points, led the Boilermakers to the national championship and was named the Helms Athletic Foundation College Basketball Player of the Year.

An English major and academic achievement honoree, Wooden was wooed by New York publishing companies that wanted him to be their Midwestern representative. He, instead, opted for teaching, taking a post at Dayton High School in Kentucky. At Dayton, he coached the basketball and baseball teams for two years. Next stop for the man who would become a basketball legend was Central High School in South Bend, Indiana, where he coached from 1934 to 1943.

World War II interrupted Wooden's basketball career. As an enlistee he served in the United States Navy for three years, achieving the rank of lieutenant. "It was my duty to serve my country," he says without hesitation.

Not long after the Japanese surrendered to General MacArthur and World War II ended, Wooden accepted a post as basketball coach, baseball coach and athletic director at Indiana State University. In two seasons, his Sycamore teams went 47-14 and reached the NAIA finals.

In 1948, Wooden went west to UCLA. While his early Bruin teams did well, the success of his later teams earned him a place at the top of the all-time list of coaching greats. Over twenty-seven seasons, the Bruins went 620-147 and won a record ten national championships, including seven in a row. Four times his teams went undefeated during an entire season, and at one point, they won a record eighty-eight consecutive games.

Many all-time greats filled the rosters of Wooden's UCLA squads. Perhaps the best known are the two centers, Lew Alcindor (now Kareem Abdul-Jabbar) and Bill Walton. But there were other All-Americans, including Walt Hazzard, Lucius Allen, Mike Warren, Gail Goodrich, Keith Erickson, Sidney Wicks, Curtis Rowe, Henry Bibby, Keith Wilkes, Richard Washington, Marques Johnson and Dave Meyers.

Wooden retired in 1975, having achieved an unmatched forty-year career winning percentage of over .800, making him one of the winningest coaches ever.

Named NCAA Coach of the Year six times, Wooden has also been honored by *Sports Illustrated* (Sportsman of the Year and 40 for the Ages), the *Sporting News* (Sportsman of the Year) and ESPN (Century's

Greatest). In 1961, Wooden was inducted into the Naismith Memorial Basketball Hall of Fame as a player; in 1973 he entered as a coach—one of only two people to ever receive the double honor. Today, the national college basketball player of the year receives the John R. Wooden Award, presented annually by the Los Angeles Athletic Club.

While many rank Wooden as the greatest coach of the twentieth century—his record and acclaim speak for themselves—he considers himself first a teacher. He was obviously peerless as a professor of basketball, but his lessons stretched far beyond the court. He did not consider himself a success unless his students were mentored in physical, mental and emotional disciplines that applied to all aspects of life. As a teacher of life's most important lessons, he excelled, using his Pyramid of Success as a model. He tells his story and expounds upon his principles in several other books including *Practical Modern Basketball, They Call Me Coach* (with Jack Tobin), *Wooden* (with Steve Jamison), *Inch and Miles* (with Steve Jamison), *My Personal Best: Life Lessons from an All-American Journey* (with Steve Jamison) and *Coach Wooden One-on-One* (with Jay Carty).

Wooden was married to his high school sweetheart, Nell, for fifty-three years. She passed away on March 21, 1985. John and Nell Wooden had two children, James Hugh and Nancy Anne. Today Wooden has seven grandchildren and thirteen great-grandchildren. He lives in Encino, California.

© Los Angeles Athletic Club/Wooden Award

WOODEN'S STATS AND HONORS

WINNING PERCENTAGE

In 40 seasons of coaching high school and college basketball, Coach Wooden's teams won over 80 percent of their games.

COLLEGE COACHING RECORD

Indiana State   1946-1948   47-14
- 1947 conference title
- 1948 NAIA championship game

UCLA   1948-1975   620-147
- 19 PAC-10 championships
- 10 national championships
- 149-2 record at Pauley Pavilion (UCLA's home court)

UNEQUALED RECORDS AS A COLLEGE COACH

88 consecutive victories	Next best: 60
10 NCAA championships	Next best: 4
7 consecutive NCAA championships	Next best: 2
38 consecutive NCAA tournament victories	Previous record: 13
4 undefeated full seasons	Next best: 1

HONORS AND MILESTONES

- 2003: Presidential Medal of Freedom
- 2000: NCAA, Coach of the Century
- 2000: ESPN, Greatest Coach of the 20th Century
- 1999: *Sports Illustrated* (CNN/SI website), Century's Best College Basketball Coach
- 1999: *Sports Illustrated* (CNN/SI website), Century's Third Top Dynasty of the 20th Century. Wooden's 1964 to 1975 UCLA basketball teams ranked behind only the 1957 to 1969 Boston

Celtics professional basketball teams and the 1946 to 1949 Notre Dame college football teams.

- 1997: Published *Wooden*, with Steve Jamison
- 1995: NCAA Theodore Roosevelt Sportsman Award
- 1995: Lexington Theological Seminary Service to Mankind Award
- 1995: Reagan Distinguished American Award
- 1995: Frank G. Wells Disney Award for role model to youth—first to receive it
- 1994: Tom Landry Medal for Inspiration to American Youth
- 1994: *Sports Illustrated* 40 for the Ages
- 1994: GTE All-American Academic Hall of Fame
- 1993: Pathfinder Award to Hoosier with extraordinary service on behalf of American youth
- 1993: CASEY (Citation for Amateur Sports Excellence) Award for exceptional service to amateur athletics—first to receive it
- 1985: Bellarmine Medal of Excellence—first sports figure to receive it; other recipients include Mother Teresa and Walter Cronkite
- 1977: UCLA All-American Marques Johnson named as the first recipient of the John R. Wooden Award
- 1975: California Sports Father of the Year
- 1974: Velvet Covered Brick Award for Christian Leadership—first to receive it
- 1974: California Grandfather of the Year Award, given by the National Father's Day Committee
- 1974: James A. Naismith Peach Basket Award—first to receive it
- 1974: John Bunn Hall of Fame Service Award—first to receive it
- 1973: Whitney Young Urban League Award of Humanitarian Service
- 1973: *Sports Illustrated* Sportsman of the Year
- 1973: Naismith Memorial Basketball Hall of Fame as a coach— at the time, the only Hall of Fame inductee in more than one category
- 1972: Published *They Call Me Coach*, with Jack Tobin

- 1971: Friars Club Coach of the Year
- 1970: *Sporting News* Sportsman of the Year
- 1968: Honored by Christian Church for service and concern for mankind
- 1966: Published *Practical Modern Basketball*
- 1964, 1967, 1968, 1970, 1972, 1973, 1975: College Basketball Coach of the Year
- 1964: Indiana Basketball Hall of Fame, an original inductee
- 1964: California Father of the Year
- 1960: Naismith Memorial Basketball Hall of Fame as a player
- 1943: All-Time All-American Basketball Team, named by the Naismith Memorial Basketball Hall of Fame
- 1932: Big Ten medal for proficiency in scholarship and athletics, given to graduating athlete with outstanding grades
- 1932: Helms Athletic Foundation College Basketball Player of the Year
- 1930, 1931, 1932: All-American basketball player at Purdue University

JAY CARTY

I knew I was a good speaker. For 27 years I spoke in churches, youth camps and other Christian venues—then I lost my voice. Frankly, I was always a little surprised that God didn't give me a greater profile. Standing 6-feet, 8-inches, I was certainly one of the tallest people behind any pulpit, though many are larger in girth. But here I do not infer physical size; rather, I mean sphere of influence.

Among Christian speakers, there are eagles, falcons, hawks and buzzards. Billy Graham, Charles Colson and James Dobson are eagles. I was a buzzard. Nonetheless, sometimes I would catch myself thinking, *I'm a better communicator than so-and-so, but he's doing big gigs and I'm in little churches. What's going on, God?*

That's when I came to realize that my responsibility to God is a vertical relationship. His responsibility is horizontal influence. And God chose to limit and then stop my impact as a speaker, a vocation in which I suppose I was more reliant on my natural ability than I was on God.

When I could no longer speak before crowds, God thrust me out of my comfort zone and into a place where I am totally dependent on Him. He opened the door for the One-on-One series of books, even though I was not a trained writer. That was a huge step for a kid who grew up in the Mojave Desert of California.

GROWING UP

As a kid I didn't know Jesus as my Savior, but I began to trust God. I could pray "Now I lay me down to sleep," and I would call out to God to help me get through the night when my parents were fighting or were drunk again.

When I was in the third grade, a family from down the street convinced my mom and me to go to church one night. There was an invitation and my mom asked me if I would go forward. I thought she wanted to go, so I went with her. She went to get me saved. Neither of us was, but we each went for the other.

Because of my parents' drinking and fighting, we moved a lot. When I entered a new school at the start of the fourth grade, my teacher was worried about my development, thinking that being so much taller than everyone else would be bad for me. As a remedy, I was placed in front of the fifth grade class and was told to read three paragraphs from a book. I knew how to read, so the teacher was impressed and the next day I was in the fifth grade.

Early in junior high, my mom gave me a *King James Bible*. I enjoyed reading the Old Testament stories and looking up the naughty words. I always thought I was getting away with something when I read the word "bastard." It actually appears twice.

I was in the seventh grade when my folks finally divorced. At this writing, I am 64 and it still hurts.

Dad was a bookie. That's a person who illegally takes bets on horse races. He also ran the poker games in the back of a bar. I was a bar kid and became an expert shuffleboard player on the old, long wooden tables with the round metal pucks that I learned to accurately lag with either hand. An old alcoholic named Bill and I never lost a game. He would get a beer and I would get a Coke.

I knew what my dad did was illegal, so one day after school I confronted him. I was the one who cleaned the bookie joint on Saturday, and I didn't want to be a part of an illegal activity. I told him that I wasn't proud of what he did, and I asked him to stop and do the right thing instead. I approached him on Friday and he sold out on Monday, started a legitimate business and retired ten years later with a car dealership. He even married the woman with whom he had been living. I was proud of my dad and was grateful to God.

When I was 14, I went forward during an altar call at an old-fashioned style revival meeting and received Jesus Christ as my Savior for real.

FROM BASKETBALL TO BOOKS

I played and coached basketball at Oregon State University. I also assisted Coach John Wooden for three years at UCLA while I worked on my doctorate. And I played a year for the Los Angeles Lakers.

After my basketball playing days were over, I spent five years in business and eventually went into Christian ministry. I ran a Christian camp, was a church consultant and directed Yes! Ministries. In May 2002, I contracted a paralyzed vocal cord, ceased public speaking, stopped traveling and sought God for direction and healing. That is when an unexpected door opened: I cowrote the best-selling *Coach Wooden One-on-One* and *Darrell Waltrip One-on-One* while I waited upon God. And I have now cowritten *Coach Wooden's Pyramid of Success*.

I am no longer anxious for healing. I'd rather stay home, write and hang out with my wife.

Jay and Mary Carty

FOR MORE
INFORMATION

JAY CARTY

1033 Newton Road
Santa Barbara, CA 93103

www.jaycarty.com
jay@jaycarty.com

God's Word for Your World

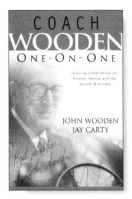

**Coach Wooden
One-on-One**
Inspiring Conversations on
Purpose, Passion and
the Pursuit of Success
John Wooden and *Jay Carty*
ISBN 08307.32918

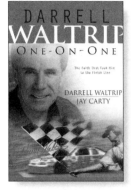

**Darrell Waltrip
One-on-One**
The Faith That Took Him
to the Finish Line
Darrell Waltrip and *Jay Carty*
ISBN 08307.34635

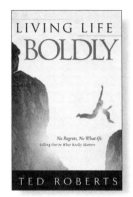

Living Life Boldly
No Regrets, No What-Ifs—
Selling Out to What Really Matters
Ted Roberts
ISBN 08307.31083

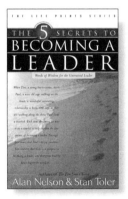

**The 5 Secrets to
Becoming a Leader**
Words of Wisdom for
the Untrained Leader
Alan Nelson and *Stan Toler*
ISBN 08307.29151

**Moments Together
for Couples**
Daily Devotions for Drawing Near
to God and One Another
Dennis and Barbara Rainey
ISBN 08307.17544

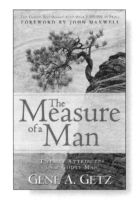

The Measure of a Man
Twenty Attributes of a Godly Man
Gene A. Getz
ISBN 08307.34953

God's Word for Your World

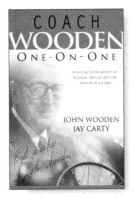

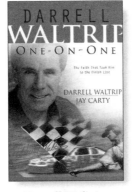

**Coach Wooden
One-on-One**
Inspiring Conversations on
Purpose, Passion and
the Pursuit of Success
John Wooden and *Jay Carty*
ISBN 08307.32918

**Darrell Waltrip
One-on-One**
The Faith That Took Him
to the Finish Line
Darrell Waltrip and *Jay Carty*
ISBN 08307.34635

Living Life Boldly
No Regrets, No What-Ifs—
Selling Out to What Really Matters
Ted Roberts
ISBN 08307.31083

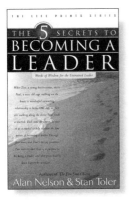

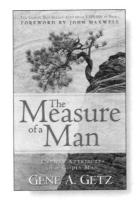

**The 5 Secrets to
Becoming a Leader**
Words of Wisdom for
the Untrained Leader
Alan Nelson and *Stan Toler*
ISBN 08307.29151

**Moments Together
for Couples**
Daily Devotions for Drawing Near
to God and One Another
Dennis and Barbara Rainey
ISBN 08307.17544

The Measure of a Man
Twenty Attributes of a Godly Man
Gene A. Getz
ISBN 08307.34953

Coming in August 2005:
Coach Wooden's Pyramid Playbook

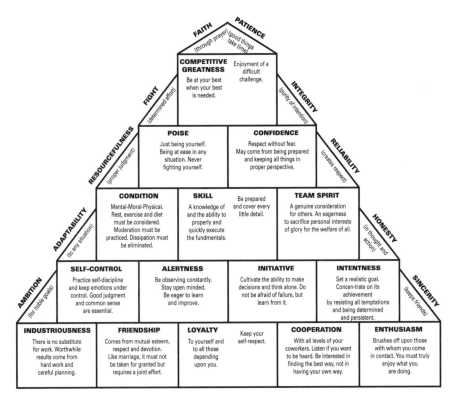